RAILWAY HERITAGE
THE
FURNESS
RAILWAY

A recollection by K. J. Norman
with photographs
from the Sankey Collection

Silver Link Publishing Ltd

First published in July 1994

The number following each caption is the Sankey Collection negative number. Requests for prints may be made via the Publisher, quoting this number.

British Library Cataloguing in Publication Data

A catalogue record for this book is available from the British Library.

ISBN 1 85794 016 4

Silver Link Publishing Ltd
Unit 5
Home Farm Close
Church Street
Wadenhoe
Peterborough PE8 5TE
Tel/fax (0832) 720440

Printed and bound in Great Britain

Cast iron Furness Railway trespass and warning notices. *Geoff Holme Collection*

CONTENTS

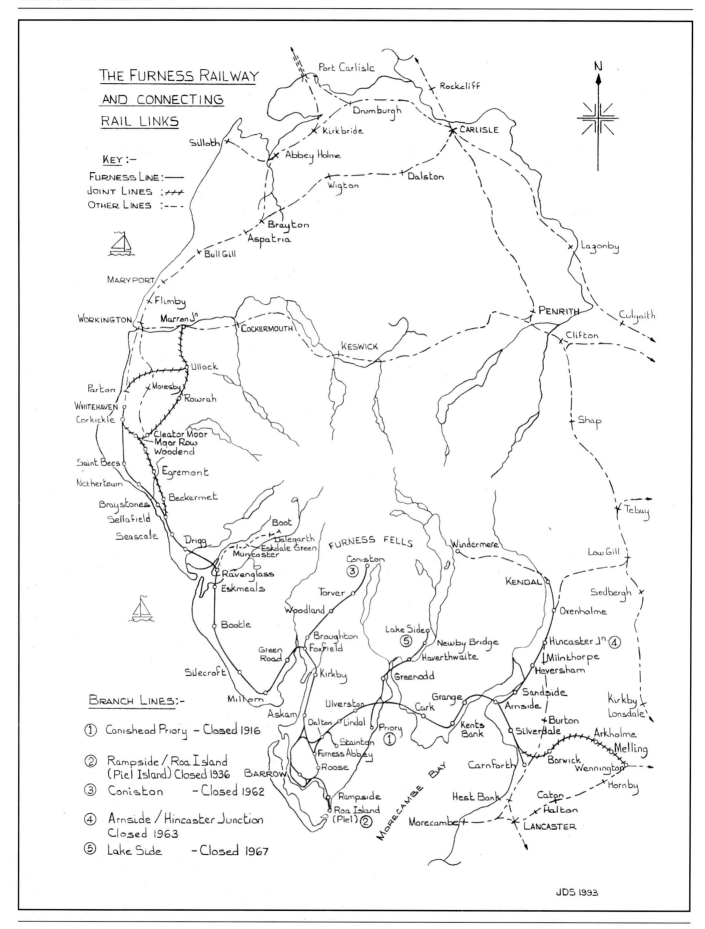

THE FURNESS RAILWAY
AND CONNECTING
RAIL LINKS

KEY:-
FURNESS LINE: ———
JOINT LINES : ┼┼┼
OTHER LINES : - - - -

BRANCH LINES:-

① Conishead Priory – Closed 1916

② Rampside / Roa Island
    (Piel Island) Closed 1936

③ Coniston   – Closed 1962

④ Arnside / Hincaster Junction
    Closed 1963

⑤ Lake Side   – Closed 1967

JDS 1993

INTRODUCTION AND ACKNOWLEDGEMENTS

The Furness Railway was opened for mineral traffic on 3 June 1846 and for the conveyance of passengers some two months later. It was built primarily to carry iron ore mined in the Lindal and Dalton areas and slate from the Earl of Burlington's quarries at Kirkby to the sea at Barrow for shipping.

The passenger services connected with a steamer service to Fleetwood via a branch line to Rampside and the then privately owned Piel Pier, which extended into the sea at Roa Island.

Extension of the railway northwards from Kirkby to Broughton was completed in 1848, and Whitehaven was eventually reached in 1866 with the purchase of the Whitehaven & Furness Junction Railway. In the opposite direction a line to Ulverston had been completed by 1854, and acquisition, in 1862, of the 1857-opened Ulverston & Lancaster Railway as far as Carnforth finally gave the Furness Railway a main line 74 miles long with connections to the routes of the London & North Western Railway at both ends. Also in 1862 the Coniston Railway, running between Broughton and Coniston village at the head of Coniston Lake, was annexed, and in 1867 a connection with the Midland Railway network into Yorkshire was established by the opening of the Furness and Midland joint line from Carnforth to Wennington.

Further expansion came with the opening, in 1869, of the Lakeside branch, a line built with tourist traffic very much in mind, followed by mineral branches to the quarry at Stainton, also in 1869, the iron ore mines at Stank in 1873 and a line to serve the newly opened North Lonsdale Iron Works in 1874. It was the intention to extend this line to the nearby village of Bardsea, thence to Barrow by means of a connection into the Stank branch near to Roose, but apart from some earthworks the extension never progressed beyond Conishead Priory, at that time a hydropathic hotel with its own golf course

and served by an attractive little station, built in 1882, which still stands. At the same time a single-track branch between the London & North Western main line at Hincaster, just south of Oxenholme, and the Furness main line at Arnside was opened to facilitate the movement of coke from the Durham coalfield to the iron works at Ulverston, Barrow and Askam. This branch also enabled the Furness Railway to obtain running rights to operate passenger services as far as Kendal on the London & North Western Railway's Windermere branch.

During this time of expansion of the railway, the small port of Barrow grew from a hamlet of some 30 cottages in 1846 to a thriving industrial town of 16,000 inhabitants by the time its charter was granted in 1867. By the early 1880s the population had risen to 47,000, providing the workforce for a wide variety of industries, including shipbuilding, iron and steel production, and jute and paper manufacture, in addition to those employed by the Railway Company itself in its offices, docks, workshops and on operating the line.

From its opening until the late 1880s, mineral traffic alone had been sufficient to provide the revenue needed to sustain the system and ensure dividends for the shareholders. However, subsequently a number of circumstances, including recession, exhaustion of some of the ore deposits, and the invention of the basic process of steel-making, which could use pig iron from less pure, more easily mined ores than the local ones, caused a reduction in goods traffic, making it necessary for the Company to look to passenger service development and, in particular, tourism to supplement its falling income.

To this end improvements to passenger rolling-stock and locomotives were initiated, a process accelerated by Mr Alfred Aslett when he succeeded Sir James Ramsden as General Manager in 1895. Existing tours and tourist facilities were expanded and the passenger catchment area extended into South Lancashire by the introduction, in 1901, of a paddle-steamer service across Morecambe Bay from Fleetwood. The Company was already involved

Left **Furness Railway: map of the system**

in steamer services through the Barrow Steam Navigation Company, a consortium formed by the Furness and Midland railway companies and the shipping firm of James Little, which operated sailings from Barrow to Belfast and the Isle of Man.

It was at about this time that Edward Sankey, a master printer who had established a printing company in Barrow, began to take photographs of subjects suitable for sale as picture postcards, which he started to produce in large quantities. He travelled widely in Cumberland, Westmorland and the Furness District of Lancashire and beyond for his pictures, which, fortunately for the railway-lovers of today, often included a photograph of the railway station in the places he visited. A reputation as a commercial photographer was soon established, resulting in his appointment as an official Furness Railway photographer in about 1906.

During the summer he sailed daily on the cross-bay paddle- steamers taking pictures of the passengers, and the steamers gave him easy access to Blackpool, Fleetwood and the adjacent Fylde villages, all of which were extensively recorded by his camera. The Sankey collection of photographs eventually consisted of more than 15,000 half-plate negatives, many of them on glass plates, covering all aspects of the contemporary scene - shipping using the port of Barrow; vessels, naval and commercial, built at the local shipyard; airships; trams and buses; early motor vehicles;

street scenes; events; and pictorial views in the surrounding villages, the nearby Lake District, the Fylde and beyond. Nearly 8,000 of these negatives still exist, including more than 300 of railway interest, and it is from the latter that the illustrations for this book have been selected.

The overall quality and definition of the Sankey photographs have provided an invaluable legacy for railway historians and modellers of today, and it has been the author's aim to present a pictorial record of the varied activities of the Furness Railway Company as captured through the lens of a photographer who was not himself a railway enthusiast.

Grateful thanks are due to Cait Faulkner for invaluable assistance with the drudgery of typing; Phil Cousins of P. R. Design, Barrow, for scanning the initial typescript; Mike Faulkner for the very fine station drawings and for checking the text; Jeff Sankey for producing an excellent map; while special thanks must go to Geoff Holme, not only for careful checking of the captions, but also for giving so generously of his time in the preparation of the text for the publisher. Without his help it would have been much more difficult to produce this book.

Finally, to Raymond Sankey special thanks for his encouragement with the project, and for granting unlimited access to his wonderful collection of photographic negatives, numbers of which have been provided, wherever possible, with each illustration.

An 1867 engraving of 'the new railway steam-boat docks' at Barrow-in-Furness.

1.
THE MAIN LINE FROM CARNFORTH TO BARROW

Carnforth station became the southern terminus of the Furness Railway in 1862 when the Company acquired the Ulverston & Lancaster Railway, which had been opened in 1857. It was the Company's junction with the London & North Western Railway's West Coast Main line which can be seen on the right of the picture, the Furness Railway operating in and out of the single curving platform on the left. To overcome the operating restrictions imposed by the single platform, a cross-over, just visible behind the boy messenger, was installed to allow two trains to use the platform at the same time.

Connection was also made here with the Midland Railway via the 1867-opened Wennington branch, a line jointly owned by both companies and which linked Carnforth with Wennington on the Midland-controlled 'Little North Western' line from Lancaster to Skipton. This gave the Furness Railway access to Yorkshire and conversely the Midland Railway an outlet into the Lake District. The platform for this branch is the bay visible in the left back-

ground, beyond the Furness platform, where Midland coaches can be seen.

The station as pictured here was opened on 2 August 1880, replacing an earlier LNWR and FR joint station and a Furness and Midland joint station. At the same time a curve was constructed to allow trains from Leeds to run directly into the new station. The fine overall roof was demolished in the late 1930s to allow construction of a second platform and buildings on the Furness side of the station which are still in use, but trains on the main line no longer call at Carnforth, as the platforms on the LNWR side were removed when the West Coast Main Line was electrified in the early 1970s.

Station foreman George Norman (no relation to the author) converses with a junior employee on the left. The fine station clock, which was made by Joyce of Whitchurch, a major clockmaker to the LNWR, still exists, although it is now operated by electricity. *2065*

Above Arnside station, junction for the Hincaster branch, serves a small seaside resort, which until completion of the Ulverston & Lancaster Railway in 1857 was only a tiny fishing village of some 20 dwellings. From these small beginnings the village was developed by the Furness Railway into a thriving holiday resort.

This scene, looking along the up or Carnforth-bound platform, features the iron footbridge constructed in 1910 by the Clyde Structural Iron Co at a cost of £258, following letters of complaint from the local vicar. He was concerned about the danger to passengers having to cross the main line by means of a level crossing when travelling to Carnforth or using the branch line to Kendal, which operated from a platform on the left-hand side of the up platform.

The original building on this joint platform was of timber construction in a mock-Tudor style, but this was replaced in 1914 by the present-day brick building, which is now the headquarters of the Arnside/Silverdale Area of Outstanding Natural Beauty Landscape Trust.

The down or Barrow-bound platform building, seen through the footbridge, is of Ulverston & Lancaster Railway design, similar to those at Silverdale and Cark. The latter two buildings still exist, but that at Arnside was demolished early in 1987, to be replaced by a simple waiting shelter. *5035*

Above right A Furness Railway 0-6-2 tank engine crosses the screw pile viaduct over the River Kent at Arnside with an up mixed goods train.

A dominant feature of the village, the viaduct was built by John Brunlees for the Ulverston & Lancaster Railway during 1856/7 as a single-track structure. It was widened to take double track in 1863 shortly after the Furness Company had taken over the line.

Further modifications were needed by 1885 when the original cast iron girders were replaced by wrought iron, the work being completed by 1887, and this picture, probably taken in 1914, shows the viaduct in that form. *5053*

Right By the beginning of the 20th century considerable deterioration was taking place in the cast iron columns of the Kent Viaduct between the water line and the river bed. As a result a 20 mph speed limit was imposed with effect from 1 January 1913.

Plans to build brick piers round the existing columns and increase the number of piers were formulated in August 1913, but refurbishment was temporarily postponed in order that the Leven viaduct, which was also in poor condition, could be renewed first.

Messrs Coulton Hunter of Barrow were the contractors responsible for the work on both viaducts, and the rebuilding at Arnside, which eventually commenced during May 1915, was completed in October 1917. During this re-building, heavy wartime traffic necessitated the opening of a special signal box at the west end of the viaduct with tablet machines to allow single-line working while building work was in progress.

Further refurbishment of the piers and renewal of the decking commenced in 1990 and has continued each summer since, when single-line working is introduced for periods of approximately six weeks at a time to allow engineers to progressively renew the Carnforth line decking and the timbers on which the rails are laid. In this post-1923 scene a goods train of 24 vehicles, including an ex-Furness Railway goods brake-van and two gunpowder vans, is crossing the viaduct on its way to Barrow. *9359*

Above The pleasant holiday resort of Grange-over-Sands owes its existence and prosperity, in its modern form, to the coming of the railway in 1857.

After acquisition of the Ulverston & Lancaster line by the Furness Railway, it was the directors of the latter company, always on the look-out for ways to attract customers, who were responsible for the building, in 1886, of the attractive Grange Hotel. Standing on high ground overlooking the village, the hotel was designed in an Italianate style to complement the 'Swiss chalet' appearance of the nearby station buildings, and it was on reclaimed land, drained by the Furness Railway Company, that the resort's attractive ornamental gardens and small lake were constructed in 1894.

The substantial station buildings, platforms and awnings in this view looking towards Carnforth have changed very little in the 80 or more years since the photograph was taken. *2804*

Above right This exterior view of the station at Grange-over-Sands also shows little difference from the scene today. The ivy has been removed from the walls and there are rather more motor cars than the solitary vehicle, registration K 487, which is under scrutiny

from the driver of the horse-drawn vehicle on the right.

Built shortly after the track was doubled in 1866, the present structure replaced an earlier Ulverston & Lancaster Railway building similar to those at Cark and Silverdale.

The station forecourt is now a car park and the trees on the right have given way to an underground pumping station and ornamental garden. *4144*

Right A 1920s view of the station, taken from the promenade looking westwards; again, the same photograph could have been taken today and show little difference. The goods shed on the right still stands, but is not in railway use; it now houses a small local industry.

The promenade westwards from the station to Bayley Lane, where there was once a small pier, was built by the Furness Railway in about 1900. Extensions further west to Carter Lane and eastwards from the station subway to Blawith Rocks, where the railway was crossed by a still extant footbridge, were carried out during the period 1902-4, largely through the generosity of one Harold Porritt JP, a wealthy industrialist who had come to live in Grange in 1895. *9511*

Above left Heading for Kents Bank, the line curves around the coast adjacent to the 1900-built promenade. Here an up passenger train, containing LNWR coaches and headed by a 4-4-0 locomotive, passes Grange's tall up distant signal, sited on the down side for better visibility, on its way to Grange station. In the background can be seen Clare House Pier, believed to have been built with timbers from the dismantled deep water pier at Roa Island. From here pleasure sailings around the bay were operated when the tide was suitable, and on occasions small steamers, sailing out of Morecambe, would call. The bandstand at the shoreward end of the pier was moved away from the railway in 1928 following complaints about noise and smoke spoiling the concerts, but the footbridge and refreshment kiosk behind it remain to this day. The outdoor swimming pool, opened in August 1932, now occupies the site of the pier, and a second pier, located at Bayley Lane, has also completely disappeared. *4142*

Left The delightful small hamlet of Kents Bank originated at the starting point of the route across the sands of Morecambe Bay to Hest Bank which, until the opening of the Ulverston & Lancaster Railway in 1857, had been the most important route between the Furness peninsular and the rest of Lancashire since monastic times.

This view of Kents Bank station from the eastern end features a typical Furness Railway country station signal box with an 0-6-0 tender engine on the up or Carnforth-bound line having the all clear

from the Up Starter, a lower quadrant signal with a winch-operated lamp. *5843*

Above Another view of Kents Bank station, looking towards Grange-over-Sands. The time is 2.10 pm and an afternoon train, conveying a Midland Railway clerestory coach, is drawing in on its way to Barrow in the charge of an 0-6-0 tender locomotive. The frock-coated Station Master unfortunately obscures the buffer beam, making positive identification of the engine impossible, but this is one of a class of 19, designed by William Pettigrew, the Furness Railway Locomotive & Carriage Superintendent, which were introduced progressively between 1913 and 1920 for hauling heavy mineral trains. A number of these locomotives, after being fitted with steam-heating apparatus and the vacuum brake, were frequently to be seen on passenger trains on the Furness Railway main line.

The gabled stone building on the extreme left of the picture is the station house dating from Ulverston & Lancaster days, and the stone and wooden extension containing waiting rooms and toilets was added by the Furness Railway in the 1890s.

This photograph was taken before the platform widening, for which approval was given in October 1914, had been carried out. This wooden extension was removed when replacement became necessary during the 1950s, and the platform reverted to its original width. *2668*

MAIN LINE. — 1

WEEK DAYS. / SUNDAYS.

DOWN.

The timetable lists the following stations (DOWN):
Carnforth (dep), Silverdale, Arnside, Grange, Kents Bank, Cark and Cartmel, Ulverston (arr/dep), Lindal, Dalton, Furness Abbey, Roose, Barrow (Central Stn. arr) (R'sden Dock arr).

And the second DOWN section:
Barrow (R'sden Dock dep) (Central Stn. dep), Askam, Kirkby, Foxfield, Green Road, Millom, Silecroft, Bootle, Eskmeals, Ravenglass, Drigg, Seascale, Sellafield, Braystones, Nethertown, St. Bees, Whitehaven (Cor'kle arr) (Br'sty arr).

Footnotes (DOWN): * Horses and Private Carriages are not conveyed locally by these trains. ** Horses and Private Carriages are not conveyed by these trains. A Stops to set down Passengers on informing the Guard at the preceding stopping Station, and by signal when required to take up Passengers. C Tuesdays, Thursdays and Saturdays only. D Stops to set down Passengers from Stations beyond Carnforth only on informing the Guard at Carnforth. E Daily until September 19th, and afterwards on Thursdays and Saturdays only. F Till September 19th stops by signal to take up Passengers for Ulverston, Haverthwaite, Lindal and Stations beyond only. G Stops to set down Passengers from Ulverston and Stations beyond only on informing the Guard at Ulverston. H A Carriage slipped. J Stops by Signal to take up Passengers for Belfast only on Tuesdays, Thursdays, and Saturdays. L Via Dalton. † Runs beyond Silecroft commencing July 13th. ‡ 17 mts. earlier from Foxfield to Silecroft until July 11th.

WEEK DAYS. / SUNDAYS.

UP.

The timetable lists the following stations (UP):
Whitehaven (Br'sty dep) (Cor'kle dep), St. Bees, Nethertown, Braystones, Sellafield, Seascale, Drigg, Ravenglass, Eskmeals, Bootle, Silecroft, Millom, Green Road, Foxfield, Kirkby, Askam, Barrow (Central Stn. arr) (R'sden Dock arr).

And the second UP section:
Barrow (R'sden Dock dep) (Centr'l Stn. dep), Roose, Furness Abbey, Dalton, Lindal, Ulverston (arr/dep), Cark and Cartmel, Kents Bank, Grange, Arnside, Silverdale, Carnforth (arr).

Footnotes (UP): *** Horses and Private Carriages are not conveyed by this Train on Mondays. A Stops to set down Passengers on informing the Guard at the preceding stopping station, and by signal to take up Passengers. C Tuesdays, Thursdays and Saturdays only. E Daily until Sept. 19th, and afterwards on Thursdays and Saturdays only. G Stops to set down Passengers from Ulverston and stations beyond on informing the Guard at Ulverston. L Stops by signal to take up Passengers for stations beyond Carnforth only. M Stops by signal for Ulverston or beyond on Thursdays only. N Stops by signal to take up Passengers for Skipton, Crewe and Stations beyond only. P Stops to set down passengers from Whitehaven on informing the Guard at Whitehaven. Q Stops to set down passengers from stations North of Barrow on informing the Guard at Barrow. † Till July 11th only. ‡ Commencing July 13th.

Above left The time according to Ulverston station clock is 1.21 pm, and the 1.00 pm lunchtime express from Barrow, due to arrive in Ulverston at 1.18 pm, is drawing into No 2 platform 3 minutes late (see the lower half of column 9 in the lower timetable above).

The Furness Railway extension from Dalton (Crooklands) reached Ulverston, as a single track, in 1854 and ran into a wooden building, sited in what was later to become Ulverston goods yard, which was destroyed by the elements at the beginning of 1855.

Doubling of the track was completed in 1858, by which time a more substantial station building, located beyond the railway on the right of the picture, had been built. For a time this was the terminus of the Furness Railway and passengers travelling onwards joined trains on the Ulverston & Lancaster Railway using a lower level station by means of steps located at the end of the railings seen on the right of the picture.

Designed by the Lancaster architects Paley & Austin, the station shown here is the third, opened in 1874, having been tendered for at £9,025 by its builders. It is today a listed building, as indeed is the 1858 structure, which was converted to a prestige motor car showroom during 1989.

Ulverston East signal box, prominently featured in the foreground of the picture, replaced an earlier structure on 10 July 1898, but was closed in 1933 and demolished, being replaced with a ground frame off the end of the platform. This too has now gone and the station is controlled from a box situated a few hundred yards from the western end of the platforms. *5817*

Above Main-line trains from the 1914 Summer Timetable, pocket edition.

Left Taken shortly after the previous photograph, but this time from platform level, the lunchtime express is shown leaving for Carnforth at 1.23 pm headed by 1913-introduced 4-4-0 passenger locomotive No 130.

The express was scheduled to call only at Ulverston and Grange, although on request it would stop at Furness Abbey to set down passengers from stations north of Barrow and pick up those, presumably guests from Furness Abbey Hotel, travelling to stations beyond Carnforth, where there were connections with LNWR services to Glasgow and Edinburgh in the north and Liverpool, Manchester and London Euston in the south.

It is interesting to note that while the station dates from 1874, the clock in the tower was not installed until 1902 when the Company's Traffic & Works Committee, at its meeting on 22 April of that year, asked the General Manager to obtain tenders for striking and non-striking clocks with opal dials for night illumination and to submit these to the Deputy Chairman for consideration. The clock subsequently installed still has to be wound up once every week.

The roof of the 1858 building is just discernable on the right, and the station nameboard on the left informed passengers that Ulverston was the junction station for the Lakeside (Windermere) and Conishead branches. *5816*

Above A view from the western end of Ulverston station with a Carnforth-bound train in the up platform and milk churns being man-handled across the down, Barrow-bound line.

The need for an extension of the railway beyond Ulverston was recognised as early as 1850, and when the Ulverston & Lancaster Railway was given the Royal Assent on 25 July 1851 there were celebrations in the town that included the ringing of church bells.

Opened as a single line only for goods traffic on 10 August 1857 and for passengers on the 26th of the same month, trains on the new railway were worked by locomotives and rolling-stock on loan from the Furness Company. By 1860 the two systems had been integrated and in May 1862 the Furness Company purchased the Ulverston & Lancaster Railway, at the same time buying the Ulverston Canal. The island platform between the two lines was to allow easy interchange of passengers between main-line trains and those operating on the Lakeside branch. *5828*

Left The train in No 1 platform at Ulverston, on its way to Barrow, carries a through LNWR carriage from Manchester to Whitehaven, which can be seen on the right of the picture at the rear of the train. These through carriages were conveyed on one morning and one afternoon train, the morning carriage leaving Manchester Exchange at 10.15 am, reaching Barrow at 1.11 pm and Whitehaven at 2.53 pm, while the afternoon service operated from Manchester Victoria, departing at 2.55 pm, arriving in Barrow at 5.42 pm and Whitehaven at 7.10 pm.

In the opposite direction the coaches left Whitehaven at 11.40 am and 2.40 pm, arriving in Manchester at 4.15 pm and 7.30 pm respectively.

The station refreshment room was situated on this platform and can be seen on the left of the picture. It survived until just after the Second World War and was demolished in around 1960, although its outline can still be seen on the platform. *5824*

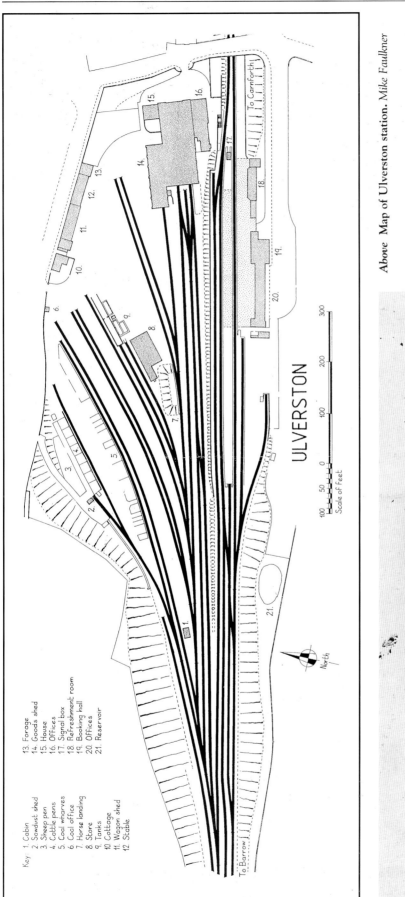

Key: 1. Cabin
2. Sawdust shed
3. Sheep pen
4. Cattle pens
5. Coal wharves
6. Coal office
7. Horse landing
8. Store
9. Tanks
10. Cottage
11. Wagon shed
12. Stable
13. Forage
14. Goods shed
15. House
16. Offices
17. Signal box
18. Refreshment room
19. Booking hall
20. Offices
21. Reservoir

ULVERSTON

Above Map of Ulverston station. *Mike Faulkner*

Left List of through carriages to and from the Furness Railway system from the Summer Timetable of 1914, as referred to opposite.

THRO' CARRIAGES. 10

Bradford to { **Barrow** (Central)	at { 6·15 a.m.—A		
{ **Lake Side,** Windermere	6·15 a.m.—A		
Cambridge to **Whitehaven**	at 9·16 a.m.—†		
Hellifield to { **Barrow** (Central)	at { 6·30 p.m.		
{ **Lake Side,** Windermere	6·30 p.m.		
			Barrow (Central) to { **Euston**	at { 9·17 a.m.—D
			{ **Bradford**	3·35 p.m.—A
			Leeds at { 9·45 a.m.—A
			12·20 p.m.
Leeds to { **Barrow** (Central)	at { 6·35 a.m.—B		
{ 10·5 a.m.			{ 5·40 p.m.—A
{ 1·55 p.m.			{ 6·52 p.m.
{ 3·40 p.m.			**Leeds** at { 6·40 a.m.
{ **Whitehaven**	at { 10·5 a.m.		{ 11·25 a.m.
{ 1·55 p.m.—A			2·40 p.m.
{ **Lake Side,** Windermere	at { 6·25 a.m.—A		**Liverpool** { (Exchange)	at { 11·40 a.m.
{ 1·55 p.m.		{ (Lime St.)	6·40 a.m.
{ 3·40 p.m.		**London** (Euston)	at { 8·53 a.m.—†
Liverpool { (Exchange) to **Whitehaven**	at 2·52 p.m.—†		11·25 p.m.—†
{ (Lime St.) to **Whitehaven**	at 10·10 a.m.		2·40 p.m.
London (Euston) to **Whitehaven**	at { 12·45 a.m.		**Manchester** (Exchange)	at { 11·40 a.m.—†
{ 12·5 a.m.—C			2·40 p.m.
{ 11·25 a.m.—†		**Bradford**	at { 7·35 p.m.—A
Manchester { (Exchange) to **Whitehaven**	at { 10·15 a.m.—†		9·40 a.m.
{ (Victoria) to **Whitehaven**	2·55 a.m.—†		**Lake Side,** Windermere, to { **Leeds**	at { 12·15 p.m.
Preston to **Barrow** (Central)	at 10·5 p.m.		{ 4·5 p.m.—A
			{ 7·35 p.m.—A

A—Thursdays and Fridays excepted, and till August 31st only. B—Thursdays and Fridays only till August 28th, and daily commencing September 1st. C—Saturdays excepted. D—Mondays only, August 3rd excepted. †—Commencing July 13th.

Above Still at Ulverston station, 2-4-2 tank engine No 73 ambles leisurely into the down platform with a train probably from Lakeside. Built as a 2-4-0 tender engine in 1872, No 73 was rebuilt as a tank engine in 1891 and scrapped in 1919.

Seats with the 'squirrel and grapes' ornamentation, unique to the Furness Railway and eagerly sought after by railwayana collectors of today, can be seen on the up platform, while on the goods avoiding line, which can be seen more clearly in the top picture on page 16, a 20 mph speed restriction has been imposed.

'Squirrel and grapes' platform seats were to be seen at Ulverston station until 1979, and a number of these now grace local gardens (a restored end is seen above right). Today only two seats of this pattern remain, to fulfil the requirements of the building's listed status. Kept in the booking hall, they are reproductions made from fibreglass. The origin of the design is not known, but one unsubstantiated and rather fanciful tale tells how Sir James Ramsden, having his breakfast at the Furness Abbey Hotel, saw a squirrel eating nuts on the lawn and it was this that gave him the idea. *5823*

Below Such an important interchange station as Ulverston required a large staff to operate it, and here they are, 15 strong, posing with Station Master Mr E. G. Woolgar at the western end of the down platform. It is interesting to note the variety of headgear, which in addition to uniform caps includes cloth caps and a straw boater.

Mr Woolgar, who was born in May 1860, started working on the Furness Railway at Ulverston on 11 August 1873 as an office boy earning 6s 6d per week. By 1878, as a clerk, this had risen to 20 shillings (£1.00) per week, and on his appointment as Station Master in 1896 his salary was £90 per annum. Mr Woolgar remained as Station Master at Ulverston until his retirement on 1 August 1919, when he was earning £450 per annum, a sizable salary in those far-off years, and it is possible that this photograph was taken to mark that occasion.

This end of the platform and the rooms behind are now occupied by a privately owned entertainment club appropriately named 'Buffers'. *5832*

Right A seven-coach passenger train bound for Barrow passes the western end of Lindal Ore Sidings behind 4-4-0 passenger locomotive No 133. Coming into service in 1914, this locomotive was the last of 20 4-4-0 passenger engines introduced between 1890 and 1914 by the Furness Railway. She had the distinction of carrying the highest number allocated by the Company to any of its locomotive stock. The 4-4-0s hauled main-line passenger trains, sometimes double-headed, until the appearance of the 4-6-4 'Baltic' tanks in 1920.

At the time that this photograph was taken, the ore sidings would have been thronged with wagons filled with iron ore dug from the many mines in the Lindal area, and in the background can be seen the buildings and chimneys of Lowfield Pit.

It was close to this spot, in the sidings on the right of the picture, that Sharp Stewart 0-6-0 goods engine No 115 was engulfed in a huge crater, caused by subsidence, while shunting on 22 September 1892. The crew managed to jump to safety and the tender was saved, but the locomotive disappeared and is now thought to be some 200 feet beneath the surface, possibly in old mine workings that honeycomb the earth in this area. From time to time various schemes have been proposed to locate, and if possible recover, the old engine, but to date no attempt has been made.

The locomotive number of the lost engine was not used again until 1898 when sister locomotive 114 was allocated the vacant number to allow 114 to be given to one of the new 0-6-2 tank locomotives being introduced at that time. In 1920 the number 115 was re-allocated once again to the first of five new 'Baltic' tanks (see page 61), the 0-6-0 being renumbered 70. *5849*

Below Lindal station, with its two platforms and goods avoiding line seen on the right of the picture, opened when the Furness Railway extension to Ulverston reached Lindal in 1851, and closed to passengers just 100 years later in 1951. There is now no trace of its existence, although the retaining wall on the right of the avoiding line can still be seen. The sandstone waiting shelter on the up (right-hand) platform was built in 1898 at a cost of £90 following representations from Dalton-in-Furness Urban District Council. The provision of the footbridge, again requested by Dalton UDC, was raised several times before it was finally erected in 1908. It remained at Lindal until the station closed, after which it was dismantled and re-erected at Kirkby where it can still be seen.

The goods shed, signal box and sidings are just visible beyond the footbridge, while in the background on the left are the buildings of Lindal Cote mine. Also in the background, on the right, smoke and steam can be seen issuing from the eastern portal of Lindal Tunnel, which at 440 yards was one of only four tunnels on the Furness Railway main line.

In this view, taken from the road bridge at the eastern end of the station looking towards Barrow, 0-6-2 tank engine No 108 can be seen entering the station at the head of an up passenger train. Built by the North British Locomotive Company, No 108 entered service in 1907 and carried a number previously allocated to a tank engine named *Wastwater* which had been acquired in 1875 when the Whitehaven, Cleator & Egremont Railway passed into the joint ownership of the Furness and LNWR companies. Becoming LMS No 11637 in 1923, the engine was scrapped in 1935. *2546*

Above The up platform building and integral signal box of the 1847-opened Furness Abbey station, shown on this photograph, date from the mid 1860s. For some time after the opening of the Ulverston & Lancaster Railway in 1857 the station was the interchange point on the route north from Carnforth to Whitehaven, trains entering from Carnforth and reversing out again after portions for Barrow and Piel had been detached. A curve between Dalton and Thwaite Flat, built in 1858, provided a direct route north, but it was not until 1873 that the interchange was transferred from Furness Abbey to Dalton. At that time also there was a bay beyond the up platform which served Coniston trains.

Even after the removal of the interchange, Furness Abbey continued to be a station of importance serving the Company's prestigious Furness Abbey Hotel, the covered approach to which is the lower roof at the near end of the up platform. This was also the subway to the down platform, which in the era of this picture was an island. The platform levels were raised to 2 ft 9 in above rail level in September 1906 to make them the same as those at Barrow Central station. The down loop was removed in around 1936, and the up platform waiting shelter was demolished, not, like so many other country stations, under the axe of Dr Beeching, but many years earlier by a German land-mine during the air raids of 3-4 May 1941. Passenger services were finally withdrawn from Furness Abbey on 25 September 1950. *133*

Left The down island platform with its through loop can clearly be seen in this photograph, together with the bay on the right, which housed the private saloon of Sir James Ramsden, General Manager and later Managing Director of the Furness Railway until his retirement in 1895. Sir James lived in a railway-owned mansion, Abbots Wood, close to the station.

Note the ground frame on the right-hand side of the picture, brought into use on 11 July 1892 to control movements on that side of the station. Also of interest is the arm on the Stevens-manufactured Up Home signal post with its distinctive ball-and-spike finial. The down platform building, signal box and up waiting room, all of which survived the bombing of May 1941, were not demolished until 1952. *3947*

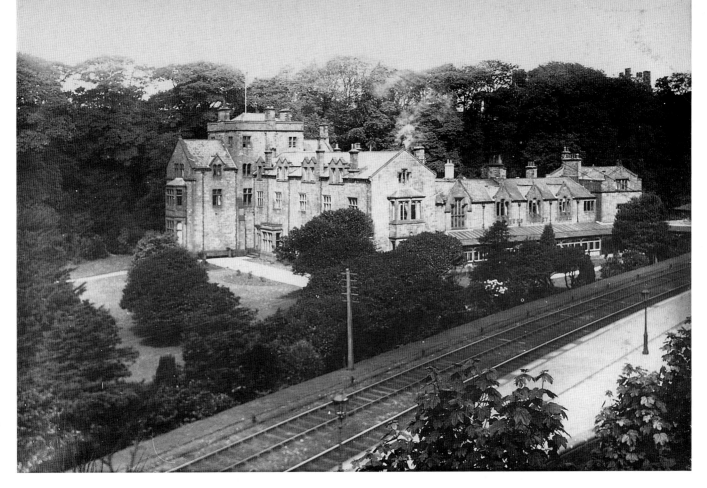

Above The close proximity of Furness Abbey Hotel to the railway can be seen from this picture, the down platform of the station being visible in the bottom right-hand corner.

Opened in 1847, the hotel was converted, by Lancaster architects Sharpe & Paley, from a disused manor house built on the site of the main gatehouse of Furness Abbey in the 17th century by Thomas Preston of Preston Patrick near Levens. The original manor house is that part of the building on the left extending away from the railway, although the square tower at the far end is an addition built during the extensive additions of 1866. The land was leased to the Railway Company for a nominal rent of £1 per year from the estates of the Earl of Burlington.

Entered by a covered approach from the station, it was an imposing building with luxurious appointments and considerable facilities. The Entrance Hall had stained glass windows, an inglenook and a roof modelled on that in the Abbey at Bury St Edmunds. A reading and sitting room on the first floor known as the Abbots Room had an ecclesiastical stained glass window picturing four monastic figures - Abbot, Prior, Friar and Monk - lit by borrowed light from a window in the roof, while stained glass in the door depicted the Company's coat of arms surmounted by a bishop's mitre; the walls of this room were adorned with bas-reliefs originally from Furness Abbey. There was a billiard room, a ballroom, whose floor was reputedly sprung with carriage springs, a dining or coffee room with a frieze copied from St Albans Abbey and a fine sandstone bas-relief of Adam and Eve from Furness Abbey, 36 bedrooms, but surprisingly, only

three bathrooms. Electric light was installed during the rebuilding following a fire in about 1899, when Maple & Company refurnished the building.

This was the Furness Railway Company's only hotel, although at various times they were offered the opportunity to purchase the Scafell Hotel alongside the railway at Seascale, in 1901, the Lakebank Hotel near the Company's steamer pier at the foot of Coniston lake, and the Lakeside Hotel adjacent to the steamer pier at Lakeside. *7387B*

Below A 1907 advertisement for the hotel.

Above This interesting and unusual view of Furness Abbey Hotel and nearby station, the down platform waiting shelter of which, with its steepled clock tower, is clearly visible, was photographed from the top of the belfry at the western end of the nave of the ruined church of the Abbey.

This very substantial tower was a later addition to the Abbey, founded in 1127, being erected towards the end of the 15th century to replace the original bell tower which was crumbling. The height of the replacement is not known, but even in its present ruined state it stands at over 60 feet. Into one corner of its 11-feet-thick walls the builders incorporated a stone spiral staircase, up which Edward Sankey must have struggled, carrying his bulky plate camera, to obtain this picture.

The pathway winding through the trees behind the station led to Abbots Wood, and this was the route taken each morning by Sir James Ramsden, as he walked from his home to the station to board the private saloon that conveyed him to his office at St George's Square, Barrow. *213*

Below Furness Abbey Hotel was managed for the Furness Railway by the London catering firm of Spiers & Pond, which was also responsible for refreshment facilities at railway stations, on cross-bay steamers and the refreshment pavilion at the George Romney museum. This arrangement continued until 1913 when there was a disagreement about the percentage of revenue the Railway Company should receive from the catering business. This resulted in the termination of the contract and a former director of Spiers & Pond, Mr Stephenson, took over the management until a reduction in revenue, resulting from wartime conditions, forced him to ask to be relieved of his obligations. Thereafter the Railway Company appointed its own manager.

In 1923 the hotel, together with the rest of the Furness Railway Company, passed into the ownership of the London Midland & Scottish Railway, which continued to operate it until 1937 when it was unable to negotiate a mutually satisfactory rental with the Cavendish Estates, owners of the land on which the hotel stood. As a result the hotel closed in 1938 and stood empty until the following year when it was requisitioned by the military at the outbreak of war, to become the gun control centre for the anti-aircraft defences of Barrow. Badly damaged in the air raid that demolished part of Furness Abbey station, it was never re-built and was finally pulled down in the mid-1950s. Only the Tavern, seen at the right-hand end of the hotel in the upper picture on the previous page, which used to house the station's refreshment rooms, now remains, the rest of the site being used today as a car park for visitors to Furness Abbey.

The picture shows the hotel staff posed on the lawn in front of the bay window of the drawing room, and was probably taken in about 1910 during Spiers & Pond's period of management. *7912*

2.
BARROW-IN-FURNESS

Top right The approach road to Barrow Central station with its gates (closed on one day each year to maintain private road status) was photographed on a snowy morning in November 1915.

The notices on the hoardings on the right advertise excursions to Blackpool (by train, as the cross-bay steamers had been terminated because of the war), Ravenglass, for the newly opened Narrow Gauge Railway to Eskdale, and Whitehaven.

The approach road left Barrow's Abbey Road at its junction with Holker Street and Rawlinson Street, making an awkward five-road intersection which, even with the introduction of traffic lights in the 1930s, became more and more hazardous as the volume of motor traffic increased over the years. In recent times the junction has been simplified by moving the station approach entrance into Holker Street. For a number of years following the bombing during the war, the station bookstall, previously sited on No 1 platform, was moved to occupy a site just beyond the gate on the left and remained there until the entrance was moved into Holker Street.

The area to the left of the picture, which used to hold two carriage storage sidings known as 'Duke sidings', is, apart from a short stub behind the present station's car park, now occupied by a Ford motor car dealership. *3795*

excursion booking office, which had a roof to match that of the glass case housing 'Coppernob'; the vehicle shelter over the station entrance was erected in 1898 at a cost of £386. *95*

Bottom right In this closer view of the station from the approach, 0-4-0 locomotive No 3, preserved and put on display in about 1902, can be seen in its glass case (see also page 78). 'Coppernob', as it is known, is now part of the National Collection.

In those traffic-free times children could play on the road in front of the station without fear of injury from the horse-drawn cabs waiting for passengers. But even in those early days a simple form of traffic control was being imposed, with incoming cabs being diverted to the left of the lamp standards.

The wooden archway in the railings on the extreme right of the picture led to the

Below An armed soldier with fixed bayonet, wearing his Great War campaign medals, stands guard at the entrance to Barrow Central station during the railway strike of 1919. In addition to a board behind the guard that draws attention to a provisional train service commencing on Friday 3 October 1919 there are other interesting posters. On the left the promenade at Grange-Over-Sands is the subject, while at the Lakeside station refreshment pavilion hot and cold lunches are advertised as being served daily from 12.00 to 2.30 pm, cost 2s 6d, and afternoon teas served between 4.00 and 6.00 pm, at a price of 1 shilling per head.

Notice is also given of a New Express Train running on Mondays and Saturdays only, departing from Barrow at 8.20 and calling at Ulverston and Grange, arriving in Carnforth at 9.30, where connections to Carlisle, Manchester and London Euston could be made.

It is interesting to compare this service with a recent timetable that lists a diesel train leaving Barrow at 8.15, calling at all stations and arriving in Carnforth at 9.07, a saving of 18 minutes over the express timings of 1919, proving that services have improved during the last 74 years. *7511*

Below A sun-dappled view of the booking hall shows the ornate roof and decorative frieze in the brickwork. The picture can be dated by the notices on the right, one of which advertises the introduction of a new service to the Midland and North Eastern Lines in 1920, while on the extreme left a poster draws attention to a rugby football match between Leigh and Barrow to be played at Little Park, Roose, on Saturday 12 February 1921, kicking off at 3.00 pm.

There are separate windows for 1st and 3rd Class passengers and it can be seen that illumination by electric light has been introduced by this time. *7375*

Above In the days when railway tickets were punched and collected at stations instead of on trains as they are today, a Furness Railway Inspector poses proudly at the ticket barrier on No 1 platform of Barrow Central station.

Beyond the sliding gates is a glimpse of the booking hall, while a poster advertising the opening of the new refreshment room at Seascale (see page 57) dates this picture as being taken in 1913, the construction of the Seascale refreshment room having been authorised by the Company's Traffic & Works Committee at its meeting on 27 May of that year. The function of this Committee, which met monthly, usually in Barrow, was to deal with matters directly concerning the running of the railway, while decisions regarding policy and capital expenditure were dealt with by the Board of Directors who met usually in London. *3919*

Right The interior of the left luggage office on platform 1 of Central station shows typical baggage of the day - Gladstone bags, wicker baskets and portmanteaus have been deposited, together with a quartet of bicycles. The porter in charge stares wide-eyed as he tries to keep still during the time exposure which would have been required to take this interior photograph on the relatively slow photographic plates of that time. *3923*

Left Barrow Central station, opened on 1 June 1882, was the third station to serve passengers to and from Barrow. The first, a wooden platform at the quaintly named Rabbit Point, not far from the site of the present St George's church, was opened in 1846, to be followed in 1862 by a larger brick-built station in St George's Square (see page 35). This remained in use until a loop line, from Salthouse Junction to Thwaite Flat Junction, was installed, which, passing close to the centre of the town, offered a more suitable location for Barrow's main passenger station.

At the time of opening, the buildings on No 1 platform were of a temporary nature, the offices, waiting and refreshment rooms seen to the left of this picture not being built until 1898, at which time the decision was taken to install electric light in the refreshment rooms, waiting rooms and offices on both platforms.

The time on the station clock is 12.50, and passengers are gathering with their luggage, together with several milk churns, to await the arrival of the lunchtime Carnforth to Whitehaven express. *3689*

Below left This picture was taken from the same view point but 20 minutes later, at 1.10 pm, and shows 4-4-0 passenger locomotive No 133 arriving, on time, with the 11.40 am express from Whitehaven. An interesting footnote on the timetable states that this train did not convey horses and private carriages. Leaving Barrow at 1.15 pm and calling only at Ulverston and Grange, it was timed to arrive at Carnforth at 2.12 pm. All eyes are on the incoming train except for those of the youthful refreshment trolley attendant who has obviously seen this event many times and is much more interested in the camera. *3688*

Top right In addition to the two covered platforms seen in the previous illustration, Barrow Central had a through loop on the down side, served by platform 3, and there was also an up bay at the southern end of No 2 platform. This was used by trains running on the Piel branch, which can be seen in the illustration on page 116.

Platform 4, shown here, came into use on 5 May 1907, costing £3,640 to build with its subway access, waiting shelter and gents toilet. However, this picture was taken many years later, in 1938, when a football special was about to leave Barrow for Wembley, carrying supporters of Barrow Rugby League Football Club to watch their team, which had reached the final of the Rugby League Challenge Trophy for the first time. Unfortunately Barrow fell at the last hurdle, losing the match to Salford. Surprisingly for an excursion train, the carriage stock is of late manufacture, the left-hand vehicle being a post-1934 Stanier design. *TP 180*

Above A detachment of the troops used to guard the various railway premises in Barrow during the railway strike of 1919 parades for the camera at the southern end of Central station. Behind the troops are the No 1 platform signals, home and distant arms on a common post with winch-operated lamps. On platform 2 shadowy figures can be seen, and one wonders if these are striking railwaymen or volunteers waiting to load the large number of milk kits on to a train.

The interesting enamel signs advertise a wide range of commodities including Wood Milne Rubber Heels, Brand's Essence of Beef, Venos Cough Cure, Mazawattee Tea and Onoto, The Pen That Fills Itself. On the end wall of platform 2 beneath the Lifebuoy Soap advertisement is the well-known jingle 'They Came as a Boon and a Blessing to men, The Pickwick, the Owl and the Waverley Pen'. *7512*

Below An express train from the north, headed by 4-4-0 passenger engine No 130, built in 1913, stands in platform 2 at Barrow Central station, in a picture that shows to good advantage the fine, mock-Tudor facade and overall roof of the structure, opened on 1 June 1882.

The event took place, according to a report in the *Barrow Times* of Saturday 3 June, without formality and merited only a single paragraph, inserted in a column with the general heading 'Passing Notes'. The report does, however, record a more than passing interest in the new station by the townsfolk of Barrow, stating that 'during the day a large number of persons inspected the station and alto-gether Abbey Road presented an appearance of animation hitherto unknown to this locality'.

The first train from the south to arrive at the new station was the 4.40 am from Carnforth, due to arrive at 5.40 am, which, according to the newspaper, arrived a few minutes late, carrying a number of excursionists from Manchester. This train then continued to Whitehaven, timed to leave at 5.45 am, while the first train south, which only ran as far as Ulverston, departed at 6.00 am, arriving at its destination at 6.28 am. The *Barrow Times* reported this train as carrying a large crowd of passengers 'in search of business and pleasure at the hiring fair at that town'.

Barrow Central remained in this form until it was destroyed by German bombs during an air raid on 7 May 1941, and, replaced by a new structure in the late 1950s, is now simply known as Barrow. *3701*

Below A 4-6-4 tank engine, probably No 119, accelerates away from Central station with a Carnforth-bound passenger train, the first three coaches of which appear to be LNWR West Coast Joint Stock vehicles, while in the loop through No 3 platform a goods train, headed by an 0-6-0 mineral engine, its number unfortunately obscured by a hose-pipe draped across it, waits for the passenger to clear the main line before proceeding.

Compare the length of the left-hand platform with the previous view - the extension took place in 1915, the platform being lengthened by 125 feet, while at the same time the up (right-hand) platform was extended by 71 feet to allow engines to take water without having to uncouple from their trains and run forward to the water column. *7390*

A lunchtime express bound for Carnforth, conveying through coaches for London Euston, is about to leave No 2 platform in the charge of two immaculately groomed 4-4-0 passenger locomotives in about 1915.

The pilot, No 33, is one of a batch of six such engines that first entered service in 1896, while the train engine, No 130, is a later and more powerful locomotive, one of four similar engines, costing £3,670 each, first introduced in 1913. No 130 became LMS No 10185 at the Grouping in 1923 when the Furness Railway was absorbed by the London Midland & Scottish Railway Company, and was scrapped in 1933.

An interesting signal that permitted movement in the up direction from the down, No 1, platform can be seen in the foreground in this and the previous picture. Built from sections of rail, the short signal post has a distinctly home-made appearance, and was in fact manufactured in the blacksmiths' shop of the Furness Railway workshops. The ground signal to the left of the post was made by Stevens & Sons of London. *3702*

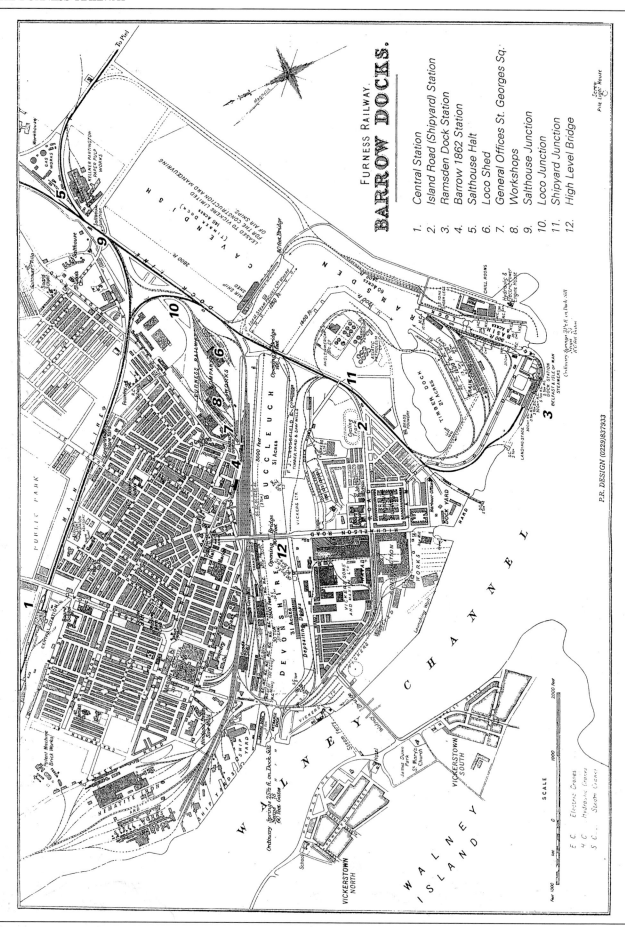

FURNESS RAILWAY.
BARROW DOCKS.

1. Central Station
2. Island Road (Shipyard) Station
3. Ramsden Dock Station
4. Barrow 1862 Station
5. Salthouse Halt
6. Loco Shed
7. General Offices St. Georges Sq.
8. Workshops
9. Salthouse Junction
10. Loco Junction
11. Shipyard Junction
12. High Level Bridge

P.R. DESIGN (0229)837933

Map of Barrow Docks.

Right Shipyard station, one of two stations on Barrow Island, the other being at Ramsden Dock, was opened on 1 May 1899. Built at the request of Vickers Sons & Maxim to bring in workmen, who came from as far afield as Millom in the north and Grange-over-Sands in the south (there was also a service from Coniston), it originally consisted of a single platform, erected at a cost of £550, on an existing goods line serving the works through exchange sidings in what was later to become Bridge Road. Never intended for general public use, it served more than 1,700 workers daily in 1901. The second platform and cross-over were installed in 1915, at which time the signal box, fitted with block instruments, was opened to replace an original ground frame. The left-hand platform was used by the Grange train and the Millom train operated from that on the right. This picture and the one below can probably be dated in the early 1920s - an early motor car is visible crossing the tracks on its way from Anchor Road to Dunbar Street. This crossing was at one time controlled by a cross-bar signal. *A323*

Below The railings and gates, seen open in this photograph and closed in the previous one, were erected at a cost of £100 in 1915, by which time the station was in limited use for the general public. Sunday school trips were run, together with excursions to Rampside and Roa Island during the summer months, while during the winter special trains took supporters of Barrow Rugby League Football Club to Roose station in the days when the Club's headquarters were at Little Park there. The structure partially visible in the left foreground was an old coach body, converted for use as a booking office for the excursion trains. Services for workmen continued to operate until the closure of Buccleuch Dock bridge on 31 December 1966 forced their termination. *A320*

Above The other station on Barrow Island, at Ramsden Dock, can be seen here beyond the Barrow Steam Navigation Company's steamer *Duchess of Devonshire*, which operated a service to the Isle of Man during the summer months and sailed between Barrow and Belfast in the winter. Opened on 1 June 1881, Ramsden Dock passenger station was built to deal with the boat train traffic transferred from Piel Pier when the deep water berth was constructed in Walney Channel. Subsequently the station was extensively used in connection with the Railway Company's Lakeland Tours and it was here that holidaymakers from the Fylde, after crossing Morecambe Bay by paddle-steamer, transferred to the train to continue their tour. This traffic ceased at the outbreak of the Great War in September 1914 and never really resumed, although an unsuccessful attempt was made to revive it in the late summer of 1922, using the screw steamer *Robina*, chartered from its owners W. A. & P. Cordingley. Used only occasionally thereafter for excursions, Ramsden Dock station was finally closed and pulled down in 1936. *299*

Below At the time of the opening of the Furness Railway in 1846 the General Offices of the Company were housed in the westernmost of the railway-built cottages in Salthouse Road.

Building of new, more commodious premises began in the early 1850s on a site excavated into the south-western slopes of Rabbit Hill, adjacent to the early station, and by 1855 the southern portion of the building together with the clock tower had been erected. Completion was not until 1864, a date commemorated on a carved lintel surmounting a mullioned upper floor window which fortunately has survived, but is not visible on this photograph.

The office building continued in use until 1966 and fulfilled a number of different roles during the many rationalisation exercises carried out after the nationalisation of Britain's railways in 1948. It was the Divisional Office when the Barrow Division was created in 1958, later becoming the headquarters of the Divisional Manager when the Barrow and Carlisle Divisions merged in 1964. By 1966, however, further restructuring saw the Barrow Division joining with Preston, and after 120 years railway management left Barrow. The offices finally closed in March 1966 with partial demolition following ten years later, in March 1976, in connection with a Council scheme to strengthen the retaining wall for nearby Salthouse Road. Complete demolition followed in August 1978, when the courts of Barrow Squash Club were built on the site. *60*

Above The view from the clock tower of the General Offices across St George's Square shows the 1862 station building with the bricked-up portals of the former train shed just visible on the left of the building. By 1872 this station, known after 1881 as Barrow Town, was becoming inadequate and was enlarged by the conversion of a nearby carriage shed into arrival platforms. Both parts closed when Barrow Central station opened on 1 June 1882, but both are still standing.

The illustrated structure, now a Grade 2 listed building, is virtually unchanged, although for many years it has had no association with the working railway apart from a railwaymen's club being housed in one part of it. The converted carriage shed, after being used as a drill hall for the local Territorial Army unit, an Exhibition centre, a skating rink, a dance hall and a ten pin bowling alley, is now, in a greatly altered form, the home of the social club of a local factory. The picture can be dated by the vessel beneath the Vickers crane in Buccleuch Dock. This is the Cunard liner *Caronia*, which came to Barrow in 1924 for a complete refit. *A192*

Above right Troops guard the General Offices in 1919 in a picture that shows the entrance gates in St George's Square, the gate-posts being surmounted by two impressive lanterns. The carved window lintel commemorating the completion of the building in 1864 was located in the gable behind the left-hand gate-post and yet again is not quite visible.

The site is now partially occupied by the premises of a squash club, but that portion of offices on the extreme right of the picture still exists and is recognisable. The tall chimney visible above the roof provided draught for the works furnaces and was sited in the middle of the junction of Salthouse Road and Rawlinson Street, in a part of Salthouse Road known to Barrovians as Big Chimney Hill. The chimney was taken down brick by brick during the 1930s after closure of the works. *7508*

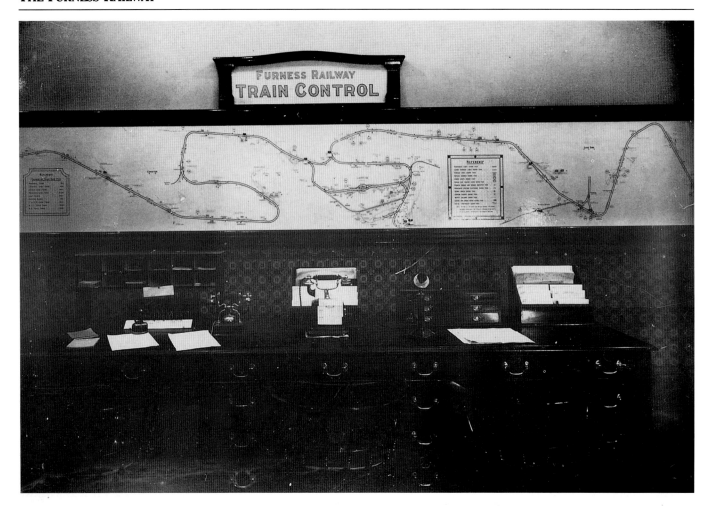

(1) The Control Office will be open continuously, day and night, Weekdays and Sundays.

(2) The Controllers will be under the supervision of the Out-door Assistant to the Superintendent of the Line who will also act as Chief Controller, and their normal hours of duty will be as follows :—

    1st Turn— 6-30 am. to 1-30 pm.
    2nd Turn— 1-30 pm. to 9-30 pm.
    3rd Turn— 9-30 pm. to 6-30 am.

The three turns of duty will be worked round each week, and each man must book on 15 minutes before actually taking up duty, so that he may ascertain the position of affairs.

All turns of duty to be rostered and not altered without the concurrence of the Chief Controller.

(3) The principal duties of the Controllers will be :—

  (a) To move the traffic from point to point as expeditiously as possible at the times required by the forwarding and receiving points, and to record on forms provided for the purpose particulars of the traffic to be moved.

  (b) To obtain the maximum amount of work out of the Locomotive power supplied, by :—

    Using the fewest Locomotives possible.
    Incurring the minimum of light mileage.
    Securing the maximum workable loads.
    Preventing congestion and standing time by regulating converging streams of traffic.

During the Great War of 1914-18 the amount of traffic using the Furness Railway system grew considerably. Steel production in the area was increased by the opening of new furnaces at Barrow and in West Cumberland; the amount of locally mined and imported ore rose from 198,000 tons in 1914 to 534,000 tons in 1917; imported oil, another valuable traffic, totalled about 180,000 tons passing through the docks; added to which were munitions of all sorts produced in the Vickers Works, the manufacture of which required a large traffic in workmen's trains, amounting to more than 300 train miles per day, to bring in the workers from outlying areas.

All of this traffic had to be co-ordinated. The Furness Railway Company had for some time been considering the introduction of a train control system, and as the war progressed the need became imperative in order to meet these abnormal operating conditions. As a result a system was installed by the Company's electrical department and came into use on 1 February 1918. Operated by three controllers under a chief controller, the system was accommodated in the old passenger station buildings in St George's Square.

The control board covered the full 74-mile length of the main line, major sidings, and all lines in the Barrow area. It occupied the whole of one wall of the office and the Barrow controllers were in direct contact with their London & North Western Railway counterparts at Carnforth and Workington to facilitate movements in which both companies were involved.

The photograph shows that section of the control board from Seascale in the north (left-hand end) to Grange-over-Sands in the south, with the Barrow area easily recognisable to the left of the rectangular reference panel. 7144

Right In common with many other pre-Grouping railway companies, the Furness Railway had its own workshops for the repair of locomotives and rolling-stock, etc. They were situated on land adjacent to Salthouse Road, behind the General Offices.

As with the upper view on page 35, it was from the clock tower of the Offices that this photograph was taken, probably in 1924. Most of the shops can be identified, the two-storeyed building on the extreme left being the Machine Shop, and the long single-storey shop to its right the Carriage & Wagon Repair Shop. Next, with a tower over the entrance, is the Carriage & Wagon Construction Shop, adjacent to which, with ventilatored roof, is the Foundry. The Boiler, Erecting and Blacksmith's Shops cannot be seen on this picture, but they were located behind and to the left of the Machine Shop.

Passing into LMS ownership in 1923, the existence of the works was soon under

threat as the new owners sought to concentrate all repair work at four main centres, Derby, Crewe, Horwich and Glasgow. The decision to close the Barrow works was made in February 1931 and all repair work for the Furness area was transferred to the former Lancashire & Yorkshire Railway workshops at Horwich.

Only the Blacksmith's Shop and main Erecting Shops adjacent to Salthouse Road have survived, now housing car workshops and new car stores; the rest of the site has been cleared and is either occupied by small local industries or derelict. *Al89*

Below A view of the marshalling yard taken from the tower of St George's church in about 1907. On the far side of Buccleuch Dock the Vickers fitting-out wharf is under construction, and the base of the tall crane, which is the viewpoint for the illustration overleaf,

can just be seen behind the barges on the left. Prominent in the middle distance is the original High Level Bridge, which carried road traffic across the railway and docks to Barrow Island, while the foreground shows a wealth of railway interest. Beyond the chimneypots on the right, with a semi-circular window in its gable end, is the roof of the carriage shed, converted in 1872 into arrival platforms for the station in St George's Square (see page 35).

In the marshalling yard itself is a line of empty North Eastern Railway coke wagons, awaiting return to the coke ovens of the Durham coalfield, and close to the white chimneys of the Barrow Harbour Hotel in the left foreground is a five-compartment, six-wheeled passenger coach. This type of carriage, often used on workmen's trains, seated 50 passengers, and more than 60 were built during the 1890s. *605*

Below Barrow marshalling yard is now seen from the opposite side of Buccleuch Dock from the jib of the 150-ton hammerhead crane on the Vickers fitting-out wharf. The yard developed from sidings laid down on ground reclaimed during the 1850s on the west side of the Strand (this is the area behind the yard to the right of the high-level roadway). In 1859 a railway line from the sidings was laid down to serve the iron works of Schneider & Hannay, which was extended to Hawcoat Quarry in 1862 for transportation of sandstone to be used in the construction of the dock walls. Buccleuch Dock opened in 1873, and it is from this period that the marshalling yard, seen here, can be dated.

In this very busy scene wagons can be identified from the Midland, London & North Western, North British and Caledonian railways in addition to those of the Furness Railway. There are also

a number of private owner wagons, prominent amongst which are several from the Featherstone Colliery in Yorkshire, suppliers of coal to the Vickers works.

This scene would be very different if photographed today; many of the buildings have now gone and in the region beyond the high-level Michaelson Road only the 1887-opened Town Hall would be seen. The remainder of this area is now dominated by Craven House, a large office block erected by Vickers in the 1960s. The marshalling yard closed on 1 September 1970 and the last remaining single track, which carried only limited trip traffic at the end, was lifted in 1989. Even the viewpoint would be different, as the crane from which this scene was photographed, erected in 1907, was toppled by a German bomb during the air raids of 1941 with the loss of two Vickers civil defence personnel, whose deaths are commemorated by a plaque fixed to the base of the replacement crane. *3932*

Below left In this companion view, part of the goods yard further to the left of the previous photograph is seen across Devonshire Dock, with the camera once again positioned on one of Vickers's tall hammer-head cranes. The goods yard was on the eastern side of the dock while the western side was occupied by the shipyard's fitting-out berths.

At the time of construction - the Act empowering the Furness Railway Company to build docks was obtained in 1863 and Devonshire Dock was opened officially on 19 September 1867 - the dock entrance was at the northern end, on the left in this picture, through an entrance basin, but the building of Ramsden Dock, opened on 24 March 1879, allowed an entry to be made from the southern end of the system, and the northern access was closed.

The fourth and largest of Barrow's docks, Cavendish Dock, was also completed in 1879, but never came into commercial use, being relegated to the role of a water feeder for the other three. Wagons bearing the names of the Lancashire & Yorkshire, Great Western, Great Central, Midland and Furness companies can be seen, but the presence of one or two London Midland & Scottish wagons dates the picture as post-1923.

Very few of the buildings beyond the yard now remain, apart from the steeply roofed chapel on the right which, after serving for many years as a fruit and vegetable distribution warehouse, is now an entertainment club, and the Crown Printing Works, until 1991 the headquarters of the 1867-established Barrow Printing Company. The northern end of the dock was filled in during 1987 to permit the construction of a submarine building hall and ship-lift by Vickers, while the entrance basin is now a car park for the Dock Museum. *A92*

Below Another view of the northern end of the goods yard, looking north-east from the elevated footbridge crossing the yard at Cornmill Crossing (visible on the left of the previous photograph above the long dockside shed). The through tracks in the centre served Barrow Steelworks and Vickers exchange sidings, and beyond Waddington's Foundry on the right were Barrow cart sidings. All of this has now gone with the exception of the three-bay goods warehouse in the middle distance, which still stands and is easily recognisable although it is now partially hidden from this side by the giant submarine build hall of VSEL. The cart sidings site now carries a Tesco supermarket as part of a shopping precinct that occupies most of the land on the right of the picture. *59*

Left Now the goods yard is seen looking south, from the other side of the cornmill on the extreme left of the previous photograph, now on the left of this one; part of the Cornmill Crossing overbridge from which the previous scene was photographed can be seen in the background. The cornmill of Walmsley & Smith was opened as Barrow Steam Cornmill in 1871; sited on the eastern side of Devonshire Dock, it unloaded grain directly from the holds of ships tied up alongside into the storage silos on the right. Damaged during the air raids of May 1941, the mill finally closed in 1967 and the right-hand building and storage tanks were demolished soon afterwards. The building on the left survived as a fruit warehouse until December 1972 when it was gutted by fire, making immediate demolition necessary. The site is now incorporated into the VSEL submarine building complex. *1012*

Opposite top When opened in 1873 Buccleuch Dock was enclosed at its southern end by an embankment from Salthouse to Barrow Island on which ran a railway line to a pier on Walney Channel. When Ramsden Dock was completed an 80-foot-wide opening joining the two docks was made and the railway was carried over on a single-line swing bridge brought into use in August 1878. By the early 1900s the size and draught of ships being built by Vickers required the widening of the passageways and deepening of the sills of the Barrow Docks, and the Buccleuch Dock opening was increased by 20 feet. At the same time a new Scherzer roll lift bascule bridge was erected by John Aird & Co of Glasgow.

The bridge was built in sections on the dockside and over one weekend, when the dock passage was closed, the new lifting portion was slid into position using barges to support it until it could be riveted together. Opened on 12 October 1908, the bridge was, because of its appearance, known affectionately to Barrovians as the 'Cradle Bridge'. It is seen here in the partly opened position in a photograph taken as construction neared completion. Double railway tracks on either side were interlaced so that only a single line crossed the bridge, the space remaining being occupied by a roadway. Declared unsafe because of corrosion in November 1966, it was closed to rail traffic on 31 December of that year. It remained permanently in the raised position for at least another year before being finally demolished.

The many-ventilatored roof of the Furness Railway loco shed can be seen in the distance. *537*

Opposite bottom Cavendish Dock, the largest of the Furness Railway's docks at Barrow, covered an area of 146 acres, compared with the 31 acres of the Devonshire and Buccleuch Docks and the 60 acres of Ramsden Dock. Completed in 1879 and entered through Ramsden Dock, it was intended to give Barrow comparable status to Liverpool as a port. Sadly, the anticipated volume of shipping using Barrow did not materialise, and Cavendish Dock was never used to accommodate ships, although it was later to play a leading role in the development of early air transport.

In 1911, after leasing the dock from the Railway Company, Vickers Ltd erected a huge airship-building shed in which to construct the Admiralty-designed Naval Airship No 1.

While the airship building was in progress, two naval officers, Commander Oliver Schwann and Lieutenant S. V. Sippe from HMS *Hermione*, the vessel supplying the support crew for the handling of the airship, carried out trials into the possibility of operating an aeroplane from water. They used a small Avro Type D biplane, the landing wheels of which had been replaced by floats, and eventually, after modifying the design of the floats, they succeeded in taking off from and returning to the waters of Cavendish Dock, probably the first time that this feat had been performed. In doing so they achieved more than did the airship, which became known as the 'Mayfly' because of the number of times flight was promised, and although she left the shed on several occasions to be moored in the dock, she never managed to take to the air.

Indeed, a young designer from the Vickers works at Weybridge, Barnes Wallis, later to become famous as the inventor of the 'bouncing bomb' used in the Dambuster raid on 16 May 1943, considered that the strength of the framework had been underestimated, and predicted that she would never fly.

However, early on the morning of 24 September 1911 all was at last ready, and Naval Airship No 1 was scheduled to make her maiden flight. Dignitaries and photographers, including Edward Sankey and apparently one lady, were assembled to witness the spectacle, but as she was drawn out of the shed, Barnes Wallis was proved to be right - a gust of wind caught the airship, the framework buckled amidships, the aft end rose grotesquely into the air and collapsed, and 'Mayfly' was dragged ignominiously back into the shed to be eventually broken up. The disaster was fully recorded by Edward Sankey, and his negatives have survived.

This picture, taken as the airship began to emerge, shows on the left-hand side the long, rounded roof of the rope walks building belonging to rope-makers G. T. Lee & Co, while in the right background Loco Junction signal box (see page 117) is just visible, with the railway workshops beyond and the wagon works of S. J. Clay on the extreme right. *1098*

Above A scene of bustling activity, photographed in the summer of 1935, as the Orient Line's 20,000-ton passenger liner *Orford* is shepherded through the 8-acre basin of Ramsden Dock on her way to a refit by her builders, Vickers Armstrongs Ltd. The gates at the entrance to the dock from Walney Channel can be seen, closed, in the left foreground.

Towed by Barrow-based LMS tugs *Devonshire* and *Ramsden*, with two further tugs, owned by the Rea Towing Company of Liverpool, controlling her stern, *Orford*, after threading her way along the basin, will be guided through a lock before entering the main body of the dock, whence she will negotiate the bascule bridge seen on the previous page and the high-level bridge seen on page 37 before reaching her berth beneath the 150-ton crane on the Vickers fitting-out wharf in Devonshire Dock.

In addition to the main dock area, Ramsden Dock also had a branch known as the Anchor Line basin, the southern side of which was lined by grain sheds. These and the grain elevators associated with them can be seen beyond the dockside cranes to the left of the liner's stern. A468

Left Taken from the deck of one of the paddle-steamers at low tide, this view of the Dock Station landing stage beside the entrance to Ramsden Dock shows the different levels at which passengers could land, or embark, depending on the level of the tide. The goods wagon just visible is a 10-ton four-plank type built in the 1880s, of which the Furness Railway had more than 250 available for traffic. *1072*

Above A great deal of railway activity was concentrated in the Ramsden Dock area, and here is an interesting array of goods stock, photographed in early LMS days. Several still carry the names of their pre-Grouping companies, and wagons from the Midland, London & North Western, Cleator & Workington and Furness companies can be identified.

The vessel in the background is the Furness-Withy Line steamer *Quernmore*, which, with her sister ship *Dromore*, sailed on a service between Barrow and New York from Ramsden Dock. *8137*

Below A train of oil tank wagons from the Anglo-American Oil Company's installation at Ramsden Dock is posed alongside Ramsden Dock Road, down the centre of which can be seen the single tramway track on which Corporation tramcars travelled between the town and Ramsden Dock station. First laid down in

1886, the tramway was operated by steam trams until 1904, at which time electric traction, managed for Barrow Corporation by the British Electric Traction Company, took over.

Immaculate 0-6-0 goods engine No 27, in charge of the train, was one of a batch of 19 such engines entering service between 1913 and 1920, and supplied variously by Sharp Stewart, Nasmyth Wilson and the North British Locomotive Company. No 27 was built by the latter company, entering service in 1914 and inheriting its number from an 1866-built 0-4-0 tender engine, which then became 27A in the supplementary list. Designed primarily for hauling heavy mineral trains, these engines were frequently used on passenger services, and all lived to be taken into LMS ownership at the Grouping in 1923; the new No 27 became LMS number 12498. Six of these engines even survived to be nationalised in 1948, but No 27 was not one of them, having been scrapped in 1932. *7547*

Above The advantages of Barrow as a sea-port, protected as it is by the natural sea barrier of Walney Island, soon became apparent to Sir James Ramsden as he pursued his policy of developing the industrial and commercial potential of the region. However, this natural barrier was later to prove something of a disadvantage, as its close proximity to Barrow Island, together with the action of tides sweeping up and down Walney Channel, were to create a silting problem not originally appreciated. It was largely due to the dredging of this silt, which in future years was to prove so costly, that Sir James's dream of Barrow as a port rivalling Liverpool in importance, was never realised.

In 1863 Royal Assent was granted to a Bill transferring the estates of the Barrow Harbour Commissioners to the Furness Railway, giving the Company the power to construct docks. When the four docks at Barrow, owned and operated by the Railway Company, had been completed, they dealt with a considerable amount of shipping traffic of all types, both freight and passenger, including daily sailings to Belfast and, in the summer, to the Isle of Man, by steamers jointly owned by the Furness and Midland companies in conjunction with the Barrow Shipping firm James Little.

All of this activity was controlled from the Harbour Office, which, when the docks entrance was at the northern end of the system, was at the northern end of Devonshire Dock. However, with the opening of Ramsden Dock in 1881 and the transfer of the entrance to the southern end of the system, a new harbour office, seen here, was built on a prominence overlooking Ramsden Dock Road and Walney Channel. Here was the office of the Harbour Master, Admiral Barnett, who was succeeded on his retirement on 31 December 1899 by Captain Wards, and later by Captain Bissett. The Harbour Office is still in use, although the cupola was taken down in about 1975, and the railway lines in the foreground, which carried trains to and from Ramsden Dock Station, have long been lifted. *107*

Left To maintain the dock walls and gates a team of divers was required by the Railway Company, and here they pose, four strong, together with their supporting personnel, in front of the Sankey camera. They worked from a small support boat, equipped with a hand-operated pump to supply air to the divers as they carried out their underwater tasks. When not in use, the diving boat was moored in Buccleuch Dock close to the High Level Bridge.

The foreman diver, on the left of the front row, Mr 'Willy' Rimmer, was born on 5 March 1873 and joined the Railway Company on 2 December 1905. Along with many staff of a similar status he joined the Company's salaried staff on 1 September 1916 at a salary of £208. This increased on 1 February 1918 to £234, and a further increase to £260 was awarded on 1 September 1919.

As well as diving in the docks, Mr Rimmer was occasionally required to dive in such locations as oil tanks, to unblock valves, and in flooded mine workings. *3852*

3.
THE MAIN LINE NORTH FROM BARROW

No 30, an 0-6-0 mineral engine supplied in 1918 by the North British Locomotive Company, approaches Oak Lea Junction and the tall Park South Down Main Distant signal with a mixed goods train on 31 January 1919. The signal is of special interest as it is fitted with gas lighting, fed from a cylinder which can be seen at the foot of the post. Supplied by the Gas Accumulator Company (UK Ltd), the system was known as the Aga Flashlight Signal, and six units were fitted, free of charge, to the Up and Down Distant signals at Park South, Askam station and Green Road station during 1914 for a trial period of six months. At the end of the trial period the units were purchased for £16 10s 0d cash, less 2¹/₂% discount, this information being given to the Traffic & Works Committee at its meeting on Wednesday 25 November 1914.

This signal, 817 yards from Park South signal box, is on a 29 ft 6 in post dating from 1908, and is unusual in that it has dual means of climbing to the lamp, with rungs on the right of the post plus a ladder on the left. The winch-operated lamp has also been retained, possibly in reserve in case of failure of the gas-powered lamp. Note also the inside-keyed track, probably dating from the opening of the line from Salthouse Junction to Park South on 1 June 1882.

Engine No 30 became LMS No 12507 at the Grouping and was scrapped in 1935.
7300

Above Askam station, seen here with a down passenger train departing on its way north, is on the original Furness Railway line of 1846. Built to serve a village that developed as a direct result of the establishment of Askam Iron Works in 1867, the station opened on 1 April 1868. The illustrated Paley & Austin-designed station building with its overhanging roof dates from 1877, replacing an earlier wooden structure. The signal box opened on 30 October 1890, the goods yard dates from 1891 and the up platform waiting shelter from 1904. In June 1900 the Dalton Urban District Council applied for a footbridge to be built at the level crossing in view of the number of children crossing the railway, and a plan was submitted for a structure at an estimated cost of £350. The application, made at the same time as that for Lindal, was deferred and the footbridge was never built.

Rail access to the iron works, which closed in the 1930s, left the main line south of Askam station and the junction was controlled by Askam Iron Works signal box. This box survived the closure of the iron works and in latter years serviced a siding laid into the new brickworks during November 1899.

Although now an unstaffed halt, Askam station has changed little today, the major difference being the level crossing, which is now of the lifting barrier type. The goods shed was demolished in the 1970s to make way for industrial units, but the main station waiting room was re-opened for the benefit of passengers, after refurbishment by volunteers, on 2 July 1993. *2145*

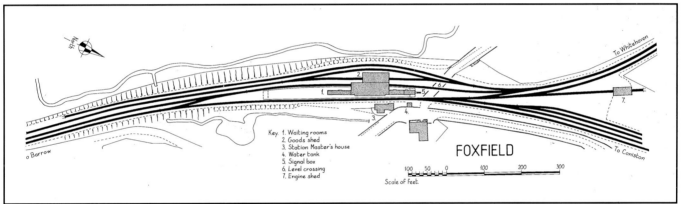

Key. 1. Waiting rooms
2. Goods shed
3. Station Master's house
4. Water tank
5. Signal box
6. Level crossing
7. Engine shed

FOXFIELD

Scale of feet.

Left Kirkby was the northern extremity of the 1846 Furness Railway line and it was from sidings just north of the station that slate, brought down from the nearby Burlington Slate Quarries by means of a self-acting incline, was transported to Barrow for shipping. This traffic, from quarries owned by the Earl of Burlington, who gave influential and financial backing to the building of the railway, was one of the main reasons for the line's existence. The station buildings pictured here date from 1904 when Kirkby and Ireleth Parish Council complained about the dilapidated state of the accommodation erected in 1848. G. Frearson, builder, of Broughton, carried out the work at a cost of £446 2s 11d.

The signal box was unusual in that, like the structure provided at Furness Abbey (page 22) it was attached to the small waiting shelter on the down platform. Opened on 3 July 1893, this box replaced a ground frame 50 yards away on the up platform that had been provided during February 1886 along with basic signalling. The site of the signal box can still be clearly seen on the north side of the small waiting shelter.

In this photograph an up passenger train is approaching from the north, but its arrival goes unnoticed as all eyes are turned towards the camera. The famous long seat on the northbound platform, which at one time appeared in *The Guinness Book of Records*, can clearly be seen and traces of it still remain. Now an unstaffed halt, all the main station buildings shown in this photograph, with the exception of the down platform waiting shelter, have gone, but Kirkby now boasts a footbridge brought from Lindal and erected at the station following a fatal accident to a passenger crossing the line. *2829*

Top An Act of 1846 permitted the Furness Railway to extend its line northwards from Kirkby to Broughton, and this it did, opening the extension in February 1848.

The Whitehaven & Furness Junction Railway, coming south, formed a trailing connection with the Furness Railway line north of Foxfield, which opened on 1 November 1850, and some eight years later, in 1858, a connecting curve between the two lines was installed forming a triangle, the northern side of which was soon abandoned. At the southern junction a station was built at Foxfield, and in 1866 the two railways amalgamated. The station seen here, dating from 1879, had an island platform, one side, partially covered, serving main-line trains, the other side being used mainly by trains running on the Coniston branch. Adjacent to the covered platform was a goods shed, and the photograph also shows 2-4-2 tank engine No 72 entering the branch platform, bunker first, with a passenger train from Coniston. A signal box was added to the north end of the platform building, which is still in use, although the rest of the station buildings have gone. The Station Master's house on the right, which in early days contained the booking office, is still to be seen, as is the water tank beyond. *4007*

Above Map of Foxfield station. *Mike Faulkner*

Above In 1856 a large deposit of very high quality haematite iron ore was discovered at Hodbarrow, and when large-scale mining operations began, sidings for the handling of the ore traffic were built at Holborn Hill station on the 1850-opened southern section of the Whitehaven & Furness Junction Railway. The founding of an iron works close to Holborn Hill resulted in the development of a small town, which was named Millom, and Holborn Hill station was incorporated into the town, changing its name to become Millom station. It was a busy station and had extensive sidings to deal with the products from the Hodbarrow mine and the iron works. The station remained much as it is seen in this photograph - where an 0-6-2 tank engine is entering the down platform with a passenger train from Barrow - until 1968, when the iron works closed and traffic from it and the mines ceased. The platform awning on the down platform, seen on the right of this photograph, was taken down and re-erected at the Ravenglass & Eskdale Railway's narrow gauge station at Ravenglass in 1972. That on the up platform, just visible beyond the footbridge, is still in position but with a replacement roof, and the footbridge has lost its sides and roof. The station buildings still stand but are not in use, and passengers in both directions are protected from the elements in bus-type shelters. Recently the main station building on the Barrow-bound platform has been refurbished and converted to craft workshops and similar enterprises. *5967*

Left Silecroft is another of the stations on the Whitehaven & Furness Junction Railway, a line that was constructed on a very tight monetary budget. This was reflected in the poor quality of the various structures, most of which, including the viaducts, were built of wood and many of which had to be replaced by the Furness Railway Company after it had taken over the line. It is possible that the wooden buildings at Silecroft station seen in this photograph were relics from the original company. The view is looking north towards Whitehaven. *2612*

Right Compare this photograph of Silecroft station, after a facelift undertaken by the Furness Company, with the previous one - even the sleepers of the crossing have been replaced. The signal box is, however, unchanged and remained in this form until 1923 when it was rebuilt, and relocated, on the opposite side of the station just south of the level crossing. In January 1907 Mr W. B. Walker of Kellet House, Silecroft, submitted an application for the spelling of the station name to be altered to the old style of Sylecroft, but the FR Board decided to leave the spelling as it had been for 50 years, and that is how it remains today. *5531*

Below A view of the railway as it passes through Bootle station on its way north to Whitehaven. The typically Furness Railway station building is one of several built to a design by the Lancaster firm of architects Paley & Austin, erected in 1873 at the time when the hitherto single Whitehaven & Furness Junction Railway track was doubled, the date being commemorated in cast iron on the station building downspouts. This was a frequently used design and can be seen on the pictures of Ravenglass and Drigg on the Barrow to Whitehaven line, as well as at Greenodd and Haverthwaite on the Lakeside branch. All except Greenodd still exist, but none are now in railway ownership. The other buildings, signal box and goods shed, are also typical of those erected as standard at country stations, and all the buildings seen in the photograph still remain although the main station house, now a private dwelling, is fenced off from the platform.

Following a fatal accident to a passenger named Bushby when crossing the line on 23 May 1907, the Board of Trade asked for consideration to be given to the provision of a footbridge or subway, but the Railway Company, through its Traffic & Works Committee, decided 'that the ordinary business of Bootle does not justify the erection of a footbridge'. *2338*

Below A snow drift at Bootle station has blocked the line and a works train with a snow-clearing gang waits at the north end of the station while the men get to grips with re-opening the route. The train includes a standard Furness Railway goods brake-van of a type not built until 1917, which gives some indication of the date of the picture. The interesting engineers' riding van, in front of the brake-van, appears to be a conversion from an early five-compartment coach.

It is interesting to note that the village of Bootle is situated nearly a mile inland from the railway, and an independent cluster of houses that grew around the railway station is known as Bootle Station. *2356*

Below On the other side of the train, looking from the down platform in the direction of Whitehaven, we see the gang engaged in the task of the clearing the snow from the tracks and loading it into the wagons behind the 0-6-0 goods engine.

Prominent at the end of the platform is the station signal box, still in use today albeit equipped with a modern British Railways-designed frame, brought from Nethertown when that box closed in 1970 (see page 61). The typical Furness Railway Down Home signal has a winch-operated lamp at the foot of the post, the rungs being used by the signalman when he went aloft to clean the spectacle. The arm would be coloured red with a white band. *2343*

Eskmeals station, opened in 1850 and closed in 1960, showing interesting rolling-stock with an engineers' van similar to that seen opposite in Bootle station. Beyond the station the line passes over the estuary of the River Esk on a 297-yard-long viaduct, built in 1867 with stone piers by the Furness Railway to replace the original wooden structure of the Whitehaven & Furness Junction Railway. The illuminated speed restriction sign on the down line at the platform end, which limits train speeds over the viaduct to 45 mph, is also of interest; the Furness Company was a pioneer of this type of sign, which alerted drivers to restrictions even during the hours of darkness. Interesting too are the Home signals in the distance mounted back to back on a single post, a standard arrangement for stations without signal boxes. Similar signals can be seen at Braystones further north and at Heversham on the Hincaster branch. The down (left-hand side) platform waiting shelter was erected in 1902 at a cost of £40, after residents had complained about having to wait for northbound trains on the up platform in wet weather.

South of Eskmeals was a gun-proving range belonging to Vickers, on which naval guns were proof tested. This was served by a siding off the main down line, controlled by a signal box that was taken down on 22 November 1992 for preservation by a local railway enthusiast. Works personnel travelling to and from the gun range were catered for at a wooden halt platform named Monk Moors, erected in 1901, where trains would stop, on request, for their convenience. *2981*

Below This view of the station at Ravenglass was taken from the up platform looking in the direction of Barrow, with 4-4-0 passenger engine No 126 in the offset down platform heading a train for Whitehaven. A 1901 introduction, this Sharp Stewart-built locomotive was scrapped in 1931 carrying LMS number 10143.

The typical Furness Railway country station goods shed can be seen beyond the platform end, while in the background are the tall signal box and the footbridge that carried, and indeed still does carry, passengers alighting from trains from the south across the tracks to the Ravenglass & Eskdale Railway. This footbridge, although maintained by the railway and allocated FR Bridge No 146, is not a station footbridge as such, but was constructed to carry a public footpath over the railway. *5153*

Bottom Here the station is seen looking towards Whitehaven in a photograph taken from the footbridge visible in the background of the previous picture. In the up platform locomotive No 131, introduced in 1913 and one of the final batch of 4-4-0 passenger engines, waits with a train for Barrow for a busy interchange of passengers. Stored on the siding leading to the goods shed is a 1906-built cattle van, its lower sides liberally coated with lime, while on the down line an up goods train, running wrong line, is waiting for the passenger train to clear the station before crossing to its correct road.

Ravenglass station opened in 1849 when the Whitehaven & Furness Junction Railway had reached this point on its way south to join with the Furness Railway at Broughton. The track was doubled in 1872 after the Furness Company acquired the line, which allowed the station as seen here to be constructed in 1873.

All buildings in this scene still exist, passing into the ownership of the Ravenglass & Eskdale Railway when British Railways made Ravenglass an unmanned halt in 1967. The main station building is now the 'Ratty Arms', the goods shed is a workshop and the up platform waiting shelter now houses a museum. *5662*

The Ravenglass & Eskdale Railway

Right Although never a part of the Furness Railway, it seems sensible to break the journey northwards at Ravenglass to take a brief look at the history and operation of the narrow gauge railway that runs along Eskdale, from the sea at Ravenglass to the head of the valley.

This railway opened in 1875 as a 3-foot-gauge line intended primarily to transport iron ore, mined at the head of the Esk valley, to the coast at Ravenglass for shipping. Known locally as the 'Ratty', it was never a very profitable venture but struggled on, carrying a variety of minerals and passengers, and surviving more than one crisis, until 30 April 1913 when it was finally closed. It lay unused and falling into decay until 1915 when an enterprise known as 'Narrow Gauge Railways', operators of 15-inch-gauge pleasure lines at seaside resorts, leased the railway and re-arranged the tracks to the narrower gauge. Passenger services as far as Muncaster Mill were resumed in August 1915 using the Basset-Lowke-built 4-4-2 locomotive *Sans Pareil*, hauling stock borrowed from the Company's other enterprises. Not illogically, the line became known as 'L'al (little) Ratty' because of its narrower gauge.

In this photograph *Sans Pareil* waits at the Ravenglass train shed at the head of a train. Immediately behind the engine is a four-wheeled open coach designed by Basset-Lowke, followed by a covered coach of Heywood design. *6426A*

Below Following its opening in August 1915 to Muncaster, the relaid track reached Beckfoot by 20 April 1916, an extension that

made the acquisition of additional locomotives and rolling-stock essential. The Narrow Gauge company was able to purchase an 0-4-0 tank engine named *Katie* and the 4-6-2 Basset-Lowke engine *John Anthony* from the Duke of Westminster's estate at Eaton Hall. These two, the latter renamed *Colossus*, came to Ravenglass in 1916, *Colossus* being the rearmost engine in this photograph. The leading engine was built in 1919 at the expense of a local resident and benefactor, the Liverpool shipping magnate Sir Aubrey Brocklebank, so appropriately it carries his name. At the end of their working life the frames and motions of these two engines were converted into a powerful articulated locomotive that went into service, with the name *River Mite*, on Whit Monday 1928. The station structure in this and the previous picture is a modified relic of the 3-foot-gauge days. *6426*

Below Two more locomotives, an 0-6-0 tank named *Ella* and an 0-8-0 tank named *Muriel*, both built by Sir A. P. Heywood, were purchased at auction on 31 May 1916, also from the Duke of Westminster's estate at Eaton Hall. However, neither engine reached the Eskdale line until the summer of 1917, both having been requisitioned by the Ministry of Munitions for use in the building of a large ammunition depot at Gretna Green. *Muriel*, seen here with a rake of rather spartan passenger stock at Dalegarth Cottages, was rebuilt in 1927-28 into a new tender engine *River Irt*. Of the other two tank engines, *Ella* was used as the basis of a new petrol-driven locomotive in the same year, and in 1919 *Katie* was sold for use on a pleasure railway in Southport when *Sir Aubrey Brocklebank* entered service. *Katie* is now back at Ravenglass, where it is hoped she will eventually be restored to working order. *6432*

Bottom A photograph taken at Ravenglass in July 1925 when

Captain J. E. P. Howey's locomotive *Green Goddess* from the Romney, Hythe & Dymchurch Railway was undergoing trials on the Ravenglass & Eskdale Railway during which speeds of 35 mph were reputedly achieved. Built by the Davey Paxman Company of Colchester, this design by Henry Greenly - he is seated on the tender, partially obscured by steam - was based on the Great Northern Railway 'Pacifics' of Nigel Gresley. Henry Greenly was also involved in the design of the three Ravenglass & Eskdale engines *Sans Pareil*, *Colossus* and *Sir Aubrey Brocklebank*.

Also of interest in this picture is the Ford Tractor that can be seen in the train shed on the right. This peculiar internal-combustion-engined machine consisted basically of a Model T Ford chassis mounted on a four-wheeled rail bogie, and was to a standard design of which 132 were built at the London & North Western Railway's Crewe Works during 1916 and 1917, for use on light military tramways in France. There was no provision for running at speed in reverse, so the tractor had a built-in device that lifted it bodily off the rails and allowed it to be turned around. Used mainly on light mail trains, the Ford Tractor met its end in the autumn of 1925 when a fault on the flywheel caused it to shatter, wrecking the dynamo and gearbox beyond repair.

On the left standard gauge wagons are waiting to be loaded with crushed stone brought from the Murthwaite stone crushing plant in narrow gauge wagons, and transferred to the broader gauge by means of the wagon tippler visible in the background. *9733*

Above right By April 1917 the 15-inch track had been constructed as far as the old 3-foot-gauge terminus at Boot, but the steep gradient between Beckfoot and Boot was proving too much for the small locomotives, so at the end of the summer season in 1918 the service was cut back to terminate at Beckfoot.

In 1926 an extension, leaving the line to

Boot at Dalegarth Cottages, was laid to a new terminus named Dalegarth. Here the 1923-built *River Esk* can be seen, in its 1927-28 rebuilt form with a 2-8-2+0-8-0 wheel arrangement, hauling a passenger train. This version of *River Esk* was not satisfactory, however, and the 0-8-0 portion was removed in 1931 to be put into storage. There it remained until 1964, when it was used as a basis for a new *River Mite*. D880

Below In 1928 the miniature railway station at Ravenglass as seen opposite was completely relaid. The old 3-foot-gauge train shed was demolished, a new waiting shelter built and a central island platform installed with all tracks leading to the turntable. The locomotive in this scene is *River Irt*, built in 1927 at Ravenglass on the frames and running gear of the 0-8-0 tank engine *Muriel*, whose boiler, by that time, was worn out.

A new boiler was fitted and the frames extended to allow the installation of a trailing axle to support the larger firebox required by the new boiler, thus giving the engine an 0-8-2 wheel arrangement. After the addition of a cab and tender the new locomotive entered service in August 1927 and is still operating, although different in appearance, having been given a larger cab and taller chimney in a rebuild of 1971-72. On the left-hand track a train of loaded miniature gauge stone wagons, in the charge of one of the internal-combustion-engined locomotives, is waiting to be shunted on to the gantry holding the wagon tippler. The ends of four Heywood coaches can be seen in the bottom left-hand corner.

The railway continued to operate successfully until 1939, when passenger services were suspended, the steam locomotives put into store, and stone-carrying traffic from various quarries in the valley handled by locomotives powered by internal combustion engines.

After the war all the assets of the Narrow Gauge company were acquired by the Keswick Granite Company, which operated goods and passenger services until 7 September 1960, when the 1959-formed Ravenglass & Eskdale Preservation Society, financially backed by Mr Colin Gilbert, a Midlands stockbroker, purchased the line at auction for £12,000. The present operating company, the Ravenglass & Eskdale Railway Company Ltd, was formed in March 1961 with Mr Gilbert as the majority shareholder. The new company took over the railway almost at once, beginning work immediately on bringing the enterprise up to its present high standard. D886

Above Resuming our northward journey, this is Drigg station. Until the building of the 3-foot-gauge line along the Esk valley from Boot to Ravenglass in 1875, Drigg was the port from which iron ore, mined at the head of the valley, was shipped after being carted some 10 miles to the coast.

The up platform at Drigg, featured in this picture taken in Furness Railway days, shows to advantage the Paley & Austin-designed building, with the station house on the left and the booking office and waiting rooms on the right.

The advertisements on the station wall are interesting and reflect the era during which the photograph was taken. Roans of Whitehaven are makers of saddlery, harness and leggings; the *North Western Daily Mail* cost just one half-penny; R. F. Case and Co were brewers at Ulverston and Barrow; and Veno's Cough Cure and Mazawattee Tea are also featured. *5598*

Above right Here is a 1914-18 wartime picture of Seascale station (note the partially blacked-out platform lamps) with a Barrow-bound passenger train from Whitehaven arriving in the charge of 4-4-0 locomotive No 37. An 1896 introduction built by Sharp Stewart, No 37 lived on until being scrapped as LMS No 10036 in 1931.

Seascale was just a tiny hamlet when the Whitehaven & Furness Junction Railway reached there in 1849, and that Company attempted to promote the village as a holiday resort in conjunction with the privately owned Scafell Hotel, which had been built adjacent to the railway in 1857. The Furness Railway, when it took over the line in 1866, continued with the village's development, purchasing a large tract of land in 1870 on which it set about building what it termed 'the Eastbourne of the North', plans for which included a Grand Hotel, promenade and marine walk. Work started in 1879 but foundered partly in the face of stiff opposition from

local residents, but mostly because the expected flood of visitors never materialised. Seascale did, however, become the Company's number two resort, its first being Grange-over-Sands, and the station was the interchange point from rail to road transport for passengers booked on the Furness Railway's Wastwater tour. This activity, however, did not please local residents either, even if it did bring in a certain amount of trade, and in June 1905 they complained to the Company stating 'the numbers of excursionists assembling on the sea-front, and consequent ice-cream carts, piano organs and cyclists, constitute a nuisance'. *5926*

Right This view of the down platform buildings at Seascale station from the seaward side of the railway features the Company's 'Refreshment Pavilion Overlooking the Sea' advertised at the ticket barrier on Barrow station (see page 27). Built in 1913, when one of the refreshment houses in the village was closed, this commodious building housed, in addition to the refreshment room itself, a kitchen, two bedrooms for the staff and ladies' toilet facilities. Managed for the Railway Company by Spiers & Pond, the venture cost £970 to build. It was constructed on the northbound platform because a deed of 1856 prevented the erection of any building on the landward side of the station without the consent of the then owner of the Scafell Hotel, one John Tyson, or any of his heirs. Mrs Tyson, the owner in 1913, used this deed to prevent the building of the refreshment room on the up platform, but was powerless to stop it being erected on the down side. Had the Railway Company purchased the hotel when it was offered to it in 1901, this problem would not have arisen. As it was the platform had to be widened and lengthened in order to accommodate the new structure, which was additional to the existing waiting shelter. The building has a 'new' look here suggesting that the photograph was possibly taken in 1913. *4879*

Above A post-Great War scene at Seascale (note that the lamp black-outs have now been removed) with, once again, an up passenger train hauled this time by 4-4-0 locomotive No 129 of 1901, soon to become LMS No 10146. Several changes can be seen when this photograph is compared with the upper view on the previous page; the refreshment pavilion has disappeared and the down platform building is considerably reduced in size. In addition, the down platform has been lengthened and a footbridge connecting the two platforms installed.

On numerous occasions the Company had discussed the provision of either a footbridge or a subway between the platforms at Seascale station, and in 1916 plans were formulated for the construction of a subway costing £2,100, work to start at the end of the war. In the event the cost must have proved too great, and a footbridge was provided instead, which has now been demolished. Only the very wide platform on the down side still shows where the 'Refreshment Pavilion Overlooking the Sea' once stood. *6419*

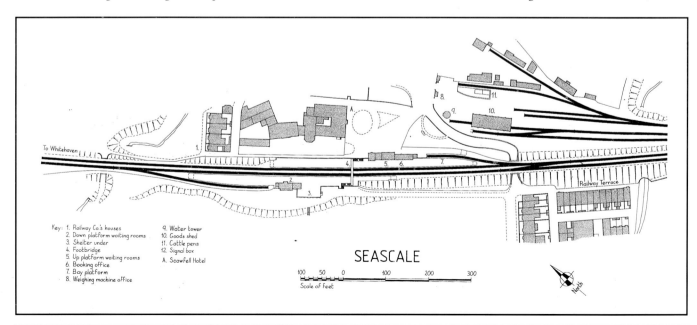

Key: 1. Railway Co.'s houses
2. Down platform waiting rooms
3. Shelter under
4. Footbridge
5. Up platform waiting rooms
6. Booking office
7. Bay platform
8. Weighing machine office
9. Water tower
10. Goods shed
11. Cattle pens
12. Signal box
A. Scawfell Hotel

SEASCALE

Scale of Feet

Above From a camera position north of Seascale station the main line is seen following the coast, in a northerly direction, towards Sellafield. On its way it passes beneath an attractive cast iron accommodation bridge carrying a footpath over the railway from the village to the sea-shore.

As with the bridge at Ravenglass station (see page 52) the Seascale footbridge has no railway connection, but in common with all bridges that cross the railway it is allocated a bridge number, in this instance 161. The crossing still exists, but the illustrated bridge has been replaced by a different structure. *5591A*

Below Map of Seascale station. *Mike Faulkner*

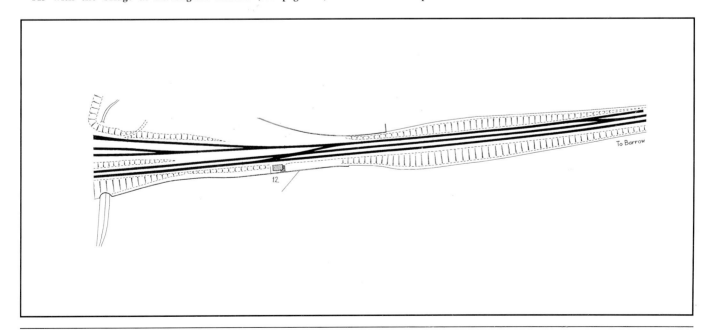

To Barrow

Above left As built, the Whitehaven & Furness Junction Railway Company's line from Whitehaven to Broughton was single track only, and acquisition by the Furness Company resulted in the doubling of the line as far as Sellafield in 1873-74. From there northwards the railway, passing through stations serving the villages of Braystones, Nethertown and St Bees, hugs the coast for several miles, and the track was allowed to remain single, only being doubled for passing purposes in the stations at Nethertown and St Bees.

Braystones station is seen here from the sea-shore, and being the only station on the single-track section not doubled for passing, it had just a single platform. The Up and Down Home signals carried on a single lattice post, as at Eskmeals (page 51), were operated by the station staff from a ground frame.

Station Mistress Mrs McGill, who had been at Braystones for 33 years earning 10 shillings a week, retired in November 1907, and as women employees were not eligible to receive superannuation, the Board granted her a retirement gratuity of £50. The station building, which is little more than a crossing-keeper's house, is today a burnt-out shell. *E913*

Left This distant view of Nethertown station, with the Station Master's house (featured in the television series *A Family at War*) prominent on the seaward side, shows the single track winding its way northwards beyond the station and along the coast towards St Bees.

At the start of the First World War, in August 1914, the 126-yard-long passing loop at Nethertown held 21 standard length wagons. A memo of April 1916 to the Company's Traffic & Works Committee described the delays this was causing to the increased traffic resulting from wartime conditions. Mr Haynes, the Superintendent of the Line, recommended that the existing loop be extended by 68 yards, at a cost of £300, to accommodate the longer trains being run. He also pointed out that a further extension would

shortly be needed, but suggested that the work be carried out as a separate scheme to keep initial costs down. These proposals were evidently disregarded, as the Traffic & Works Committee, at its meeting on 31 May 1916, approved an expenditure of £160 to extend the shunting neck, and give additional siding accommodation of 90 yards, to ease the problems.

The signal box at Nethertown at this time was a corrugated iron hut, but during the 1950s this was replaced by a modern box of standard British Rail design. This closed in around 1970 and was demolished, together with the loop, leaving only a single line through the station. The almost new lever frame from the box was, however, used to replace the elderly, worn-out frame at Bootle signal box, a few miles south (see page 50). *H225*

Above The most northerly of the villages along the Furness main line to be promoted as a holiday resort, St Bees can trace its origins back to the time of the Norman Conquest. Dominated by St Bees Head on the seaward side of the railway, the village is the home of St Bees School. Comprising only this school, a priory and one street when the railway first arrived, a large and commodious hotel was soon built, hoping to attract business from the new railway. By 1857 the village was expanding rapidly, although the hotel never achieved its object and later became Grindle House, one of the halls of residence for boarders at the School.

North from St Bees the line continued to be single until Mirehouse Junction, just south of Whitehaven, where the Whitehaven, Cleator & Egremont Railway's line joined, to run alongside the Furness line to Whitehaven Corkickle.

In this illustration the Barrow-bound train in the up platform is headed by 4-6-4 'Baltic' tank engine No 115, the number originally carried by the 0-6-0 goods engine lost in the Lindal subsidence of 1892 (see page 21). This new 115, allocated LMS No 11100 in 1923, was scrapped in 1935. *6550*

4.
BRANCH LINES

Kendal branch

This 5-mile-long branch, which linked the Furness Railway main line at Arnside with the London & North Western Railway's West Coast Main line at Hincaster, a few miles south of Oxenholme, eventually gave the FR access to the latter's branch to Kendal.

Opened on 26 June 1876, this was a single track doubled only at the stations at Arnside and Sandside. It was constructed primarily to enable coke, produced in the South Durham coalfields, to be transported to the ironworks at Ulverston, Barrow, Askam and Millom, without the need for coke trains to trundle further south to Carnforth and pass through the busy exchange sidings there.

The coke trains crossed the Pennines on the South Durham & Lancashire Union Railway line, which ran from West Auckland via Barnard Castle and the 1,370-foot Stainmore summit to Tebay.

Here they were picked up in exchange sidings by Furness locomotives and carried south for a short distance over the LNWR main line before joining the Furness branch at Hincaster Junction.

Passenger traffic on the Hincaster branch developed when the Furness Railway Company obtained running rights over London & North Western metals to run services from Grange to Kendal via Oxenholme and the Windermere branch. Known locally as 'Kendal Tommy', this was the regular passenger service over the branch, there being six trains in each direction daily in 1914, and these were used by day pupils attending Heversham School, who travelled from as far afield as Grange and Kendal.

Below left This photograph, taken from the A6 trunk road between Heversham village and Milnthorpe, shows the single line running south along an embankment towards the Bela Viaduct and Sandside. This very steeply graded portion of the branch climbed from sea level at Sandside to nearly 200 feet at Heversham in only 2 miles.

The station at Heversham, the second of the two intermediate stations, was opened on 1 July 1890 and was situated just off the right-hand side of the picture. It comprised a single platform with a wooden building standing on a brick-built plinth. The station signals, two arms on a common post, can be seen on the right, and these were operated by station staff from a ground frame on the platform. The signal arms are interesting, being of two different designs; the down signal, showing its rear side, is a conventional lower quadrant arm, while the up signal, showing its face, has a spectacle placed in front of the pivot with a balance weight to the rear. The second arm was installed on 15 October 1892, together with a similar attachment to the up signal post, and at the same time Heversham station was made into a block post on which a single-line staff-and-ticket system operated, to Hincaster Junction in one direction and Sandside in the other. The Furness Company, always economical, re-used the beechwood staff from the Lakeside and Haverthwaite section for the newly created Heversham to Hincaster Junction section, after the Tyers No 6 Tablet system had been installed on the branch to Lakeside.

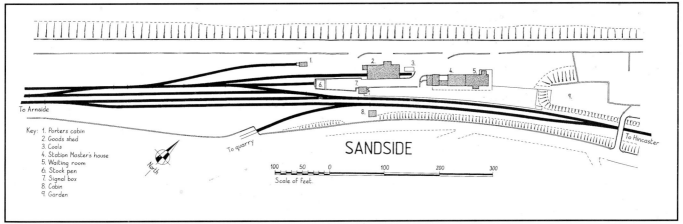

Key: 1. Porters cabin
2. Goods shed
3. Coals
4. Station Master's house
5. Waiting room
6. Stock pen
7. Signal box
8. Cabin
9. Garden

To Arnside

To quarry

To Hincaster

SANDSIDE

North

100   50   0   100   200   300

Scale of feet.

A proposal in 1900 to build a goods yard at Heversham station foundered when Capt Bagot of Levens Hall, owner of the land, asked a price of £3 per acre; this meant that the cost of the new yard, including a loop siding on the main line, would be in the region of £1,776, which was considered too much. Passenger services were withdrawn from Heversham station on 24 May 1942. *RS4*

Top Sandside was the other of the two intermediate stations on the branch. The station building was a striking edifice, in a 'Swiss chalet' style with overhanging roof; designed by Paley & Austin, it owed its existence to the owner of nearby Dallam Hall, who was influential enough to have his demands met for a station close to his residence.

Following the withdrawal of the South Durham coke trains, the Hincaster branch was closed north of Sandside in September 1963, but traffic from a nearby quarry kept the remainder open for another seven years, until final closure on 31 January 1971. The station was demolished and the site is now occupied by a restaurant. *2113*

Above Map of Sandside station. *Mike Faulkner*

Lakeside branch

The Lakeside branch was officially opened to traffic on 1 June 1869, although goods traffic had operated as far as Greenodd since March of that year. The building of the line was prompted largely by the tourist traffic potential created when the Railway Company acquired a share in the Windermere United Steam Yacht Company, which operated three small passenger steamers, *Firefly*, *Dragonfly* and *Rothay* on Windermere Lake from a landing stage at Newby Bridge. Revenue was also anticipated from the iron works and dye works at Backbarrow, together with traffic expected to generate from the gunpowder factories at Haverthwaite and Black Beck. The Midland Railway too, having gained access to the Furness network at Carnforth via the Wennington branch, was anxious to have an outlet into the Lake District to compete

Windermere Branch and Lake Steamers with Connections. 3

	1	2	3	4	5	6	7	8	9	10	11	12	13	14	15	16	17	18	19	S1	S2	S3	S4	S5
	am	am	am	am	am	am	pm	pm	pm	pm	pm	pm	pm	pm	pm					no'n	pm	pm	pm	pm
Grasmere ...dep		7 45	8 30	10 0	11 25				1 45	3 20	3 20	4 20	5 10	5	5 10	6D15				12 3	2 0	4 25	4 25	6 15
Ambleside "		8 25	9 10	10 55	12 15	1D15			2 45	4 5	4 5	5 10	6 0	6	7D15					12 5	2 5	4 30	4 30	6 20
Lowwood† "			8 30	9 15	11 0	12 20	1D20		2 50	4 10	4 10	5 15	6 5	6	7D20					12 30	2 30	4 55	4 55	6 45
Bowness "			8 55	9 40	11 25	12 45	1D40		3 20	4 40	4 40	5 45	6 30	6 35	7D45					12 35	2 35	5 0	5 0	6 50
Ferry "			9 0	9 45	11 30	12 50			3 20	4 40	4 40	5 45	6 35	6 35	7D50					12 40	2 40	5 5	5 5	6 55
Storrs† "			9 5	9 50	11 35	12 55			3 25	4 45	4 45	5 50	6 40	6 40	7D55					12 40	2 40	5 5	5 5	7 25
Lake Side, Windermere {arr			9 35	10 20	12 5	1 25			3 55	5 15	5 15	6 20	7 10	7 10	8D25					1 10	3 10	5 35	5 35	7 25
{dep	7 0	8 35	9 40	10 25	12 15	1 35		3 35	4 5	5 25	5 35	6 30	7 35		8D35						4 45	5 45	5 55	7 35
Newby Bridge Platform "	A	A	A	A	A	A		A		A	A		A	A	D					A		A	A	
Haverthwaite "	7 8		8 43	9 48	10 33	12 23		3 43				6 38	7 23	8D43							4 53	6 3	7 43	
Greenodd "	7 15		8 50	9 55	10 40	12 30		3 50		5 38		5 50	6 45	7 30	8D50						5 0	6 10	7 50	
ULVERSTON ...arr	7 25		9 0	10 5	10 50	12 40	2 0	4 0	4 24			6 0	6 55	7 40	9D 0						5 10	6 5	6 20	8 0
Grange ...arr	7 52	9 37	10 35	11 18	1 12	2 42		4 27		6 2	6 32	7 0	8 32	9A35							5 37			8 32
Carnforth "	8 20	10 5	11 0	11 35	1 40	3 10		4 55	5 2	6 32	7 0	7 52	8 32	9 0	9 52						6 5			9 0
Dalton "	8 5	9 20	10 35		12 59	2 30		4 20	5 10		6 18	7 25		9 40							6 17	6 35		8 15
Furness Abbey "	8 10	9 25	10 40		1 4	2 35		4 25	5 15		6 23	7 30		9 45							6 22	6 40		8 20
Barrow Central "	8 20	9 35	10 50		1 11	2 45		4 35	5 25		6 30	7 40		9 55							6 30	6 50		8 30
Foxfield "	8 49		11 34		1 36	3 16		5 3	6 5		8 11				11s26								7 21	
Coniston "	9 25		12 20		2 10	3 45		5 35	6 55		8 40												7 50	
Millom "	9 3		11 26		1 48	3 31		5 14	6T18		8 23			8 43	11s38								7 36	
Seascale "	9 40		11 52		2 19	4 10		5 47	6H43					9 20									8 15	
Whitehaven, Bransty "	10 7		12 20		2 53	4 45		6 17	7H10					9 55									8 50	

(Column notes: 6 "Commencing July 13th"; 9 "Till Sept 10th only"; 14 "Till August 31st only".)

† Calls when required only. **A** Stops when required to set down passengers on informing the guard at the preceding stopping station, and by signal to take up passengers. **D** Till September 19th only. **H** Commencing July 13th. **S** Saturdays only. **T** 6-35 p.m. July 1st to 11th.

For other connections see page 1.

	1	2	3	4	5	6	7	8	9	10	11	12	13	14	15	16	17	18	19	S1	S2	S3	S4	S5
	am	am	am	am	no'n	am	am	am	pm	pm		pm	pm	pm	pm	pm	pm			am	pm	pm	pm	pm
Whitehaven, Bransty ...dep		6 40				10 15	11*25	11‡25				2 40		3 35			7 30			8 30				
Seascale "		7 14				10 49	11*55					3 6		4 9			8 0			9 4				
Millom "		7 55	9 0			11 30	12*26	12‡23				3 38		4 50		8 26				9 45				
Coniston "		7 30	8 40			11 5	11*50					2 25		4 15	6 0	6 25				9 0		C		
Foxfield "		7 39	9 12			11 42	12*35		1SS			2 57		5 2	6 22	7 7				9 57				
Barrow Central "	7 0	8 40	9 45	12C0	12 20	1* 0	12‡55	1 50				4 10		5 40	6 52	9 0			10 30	12 25	2 15	4 45	
Furness Abbey "	7 10	8 50	9 53		12 10	12 30		2 0				3 45		5 50	7 0	7 50			10 40	1B30	2 20	4 55	
Dalton "	7 15	8 55	9 58		12 35			2 5				3 50		5 55	7 5	9 10			10 45		2 30	5 0	
Carnforth "	7 0		8 48		12 15	12 20	12 20	12 12	1 33			3 48	4E53	5 32	7 23	8 35			10 10				
Grange "	7 25	8 24	8 40	9 55	10 22	12 31	12 45	12 45	1 50	1 58		4 4	4 30	6 3	6 45	9 0			10 35				
ULVERSTON ...dep	8F 0		9 10	10 30	12 26	12 55	1 27	2 25	3 25			4 45	5 25	6 35	7 55	9F30			11 5	1 46	2 45	5 20	
Greenodd "	8F 9		9 19	10 39	10 47	1 4	1 36	2 34	2 27	3 34		4 54	5 34	6 44	8 49F39				11 14		2 54	5 29	
Haverthwaite "	8F16		9 26	10 46		1 11	1 43	2 41	3 41			5 1	5 41	6 51	8 11 9F46				11 21		3 1	5 38	
Newby Bridge Platform "	A		A	A	A	A	A	A	A			A	A	A	A	F			A		A	A	
Lake Side, Windermere ...{arr	8F25	9 2	9 35	10 55	11 0	12 45	1 20	1 52	2 50	2 40	3 50	5 10	5 50	7 0	8 20	9F55			11 30	2 5	3 10	5 45	
{dep	8F35						1 30		2 0	3 0	3 0	5 20			7F 5				11 40	2 15	3 20	5 55	
Storrs† "	9F 0		10 10	11 25	11 35		1 55		3 25	3 25		5 45			7F30				12 5	2 40	3 45	6 20	
Ferry "	9F 5		10 15	11 30	11 40		2 0		3 30	3 30		5 50			7F35				12 10	2 45	3 50	6 25	
Bowness "	9F15		10 25	11 40	11 50	1F45	2 10	2 35	3 40	3 40		6 0			7F45				12 20	2 55	4 0	6 35	
Lowwood† "	9 30		10 42	12 0	12 5	2F 5	2 20	2 40	4 0	4 0		6 20			8F 5				12 40	3 15	4 25	6 45	
Ambleside ...arr	9 45		10 55	12 10	12 20	2F15	2 40	3 0	4 10	4 10		6 30			8F15				12 50	3 25	4 30	7 5	
Grasmere "	10 30		11 35	1 5	1 5		3 30		3 50	5 0	5 0	7 15											

(Column notes: 1 "Till Sept. 19th only"; 2 "Thurs. and Fri. days excepted"; 10 "Till Sept. 19th only"; 11 "Thursdays only"; 2 "Till August 31st only".)

† Calls when required only. **A** Stops when required to set down passengers on informing the guard at the preceding stopping station, and by signal when required to take up passengers. **B** Fleetwood Boat Train.—Arrives Furness Abbey at 12-34 p.m. **C** Ramsden Dock Station. **E** Leaves at 4-0 p.m. until July 11th. **F** Till September 19th only. **S** Saturdays only. ***** July 1st to July 11th only. **‡** Commencing July 13th.

For other connections see page 1.

with the London & North Western Railway's Windermere branch, and encouraged the project.

Entry to the branch from Barrow and the north was at Plumpton Junction, some 1½ miles from Ulverston, while trains from Carnforth joined at Leven Junction, just north of the Leven Viaduct.

Engineered to take double track along its full length, this facility extended only as far as Greenodd; thereafter the line was single, except for a short double section at Haverthwaite, for passing purposes.

Above left Greenodd station was built virtually on the sea-shore and the up platform waiting shelter had rear windows to allow passengers to look out over the Leven estuary while waiting for trains. The down platform building, constructed in a rather garish yellow coloured brick with purple-black banding, was to the Paley & Austin design used on several other Furness Railway country stations. Freight traffic was served by a small goods shed and yard to the south of the station. *5317*

Left In its heyday, Greenodd was quite a busy little station; the Summer Timetable for 1914 (about the date of the photograph above) shows 25 passenger trains calling there on weekdays, and six on Sundays.

Top right This roadside view of Greenodd station, with an early motor car driving on a carriageway that displays plenty of evidence of the horse-drawn traffic of the day, shows the coloured brickwork and banding to advantage, as well as the station forecourt which, in Furness Railway days, was used by horse-drawn charabancs in connection with tours embracing Coniston Lake. Tour No 2, the Inner Circular Tour, and Tour No 4 the Middle Circular Tour, both used Greenodd as the interchange point between rail and road transport, the former proceeding to Lake

Bank by road before sailing along the lake on one of the steamers, and returning to the starting point by rail from Coniston station. This tour also included a visit to Furness Abbey.

Participants on Tour No 4 took to the road again at Coniston after sailing on the lake, and were transported by charabanc to Ambleside, where one of the Windermere steam yachts took them to Lakeside station and a train back to the starting point.

Winter timetables on the branch were withdrawn in 1939, but Greenodd remained in summer use until the end of the 1946 Summer Timetable, when passenger trains ceased to call. Improvements to the A590 trunk road between Barrow and Levens Bridge, which included construction of a dual carriageway at Greenodd, resulted in demolition of the station building in 1974, and all that now remains is the lower part of the up platform wall incorporated into the lay-by on the Barrow-bound carriageway. The quiet road seen here now carries only traffic travelling away from Barrow. *5343*

Above right No 21, an 0-6-0 tank engine, heads a passenger train from Lakeside across the viaduct at Greenodd that carried the

branch line over the confluence of the Crake and Leven rivers.

By an interesting coincidence this engine carries the same number as the 2-2-2 well tank locomotive that hauled the inaugural train at the official opening of the branch on 1 June 1869. Leaving Barrow at 7.30 am and calling at Ulverston at 8.00 am, a local newspaper report of the event records that the train carried 'a goodly number of passengers'. The engine is described as being 'beautifully decorated with evergreens, flowers, banners bearing the National Insignia, Union Jacks, and from the centre of the engine rose an arch wreathed with flowers and evergreens surmounted by the Prince of Wales Feathers'.

The original No 21 was built by Sharp Stewart for passenger traffic in 1864, and the 0-6-0 tank engine, which inherited the number in 1910, was built by Kitson of Leeds. This locomotive was renumbered 57 in 1918 and was scrapped in 1932 as LMS number 12502.

The single line in the foreground of the picture was a private siding that served the works of the Furness Chemical Company, and a spare section of bridge track can be seen lying on the ground between the running line and the siding. *5320*

Below The station at Haverthwaite, its main building almost identical to that at Greenodd, was approached at either end through a tunnel. In addition to its two passenger platforms, it had a goods shed, a weighbridge and a goods yard extensive enough to deal with the freight traffic generated by the nearby iron, gunpowder and dye-making industries. In this photograph 2-4-2 tank engine No 74 enters with a passenger train from Lakeside.

Like Greenodd, Haverthwaite was closed to passenger traffic in 1946, but the goods yard continued in use until the demise of the Backbarrow Iron Works brought about complete closure of the Lakeside branch on 24 April 1967, passengers services to Lakeside having already been withdrawn on 6 September 1965.

However, not only has Haverthwaite station and yard survived, having been acquired in 1970 by the Lakeside & Haverthwaite Railway, but passenger services are once again operating, after a section of the line, from Haverthwaite to Lakeside, was re-opened on 2 May 1973 following a ceremony performed by the late Bishop Eric Treacy. 4008

Bottom Map of Haverthwaite station. *Mike Faulkner*

Right The original intention was for the Lakeside branch to terminate at Newby Bridge, but before the building of the line was complete a decision was made to extend to Lakeside. The steamer landing at Newby Bridge was seen to be inadequate for operating the larger, deeper-draught steamers envisaged by the Railway Company to foster tourist traffic on the branch line, while extension to Lakeside would enable a combined railway station and steamer wharf, capable of accommodating the new steamers, to be sited at the foot of the lake.

It is interesting to note that on 19 August 1903 proposals were discussed by the Furness Railway Board to electrify the Lakeside branch, power being supplied either by a steam generating station, or by harnessing the waters of the nearby fast-flowing River Leven. It was decided, however, that the cost of this would be prohibitive, and a further proposal to introduce a steam railmotor car, which could run on both the Lakeside and Coniston branches, was adopted instead.

The railmotor, which could carry 12 1st Class and 36 3rd Class passengers, also had a trailer, with seating for a further 24 3rd Class passengers, available for use as required. Built by the Railway Company in its Barrow workshops at a cost of £2,000, the railmotor was ready to enter service at the start of the 1905 summer timetable. In preparation for this event a timber platform was built at Newby Bridge to allow passengers wishing to alight there to do so without having to walk back from Lakeside. The new station was known as Newby Bridge Motor Car Platform, and photographs exist of it carrying that name.

It is on record that during May 1905, 198 passengers alighted from the railmotor at Newby Bridge and 52 had booked from there. Despite early promise, however, the railmotor was not a success and it was withdrawn from service on the Lakeside branch at the end of the 1905 season, although it continued to run on the Coniston branch until the end of the 1908 Winter Timetable, much to the aggravation of the regular passengers on that line who complained frequently about the uncomfortable ride of the vehicle. Newby Bridge station was, however, kept in operation, although it was necessary to lengthen the platform in order to accommodate ordinary trains. This work was carried out during the winter of 1905-06, and at the same time the name was changed to Newby Bridge Platform, as seen on this photograph.

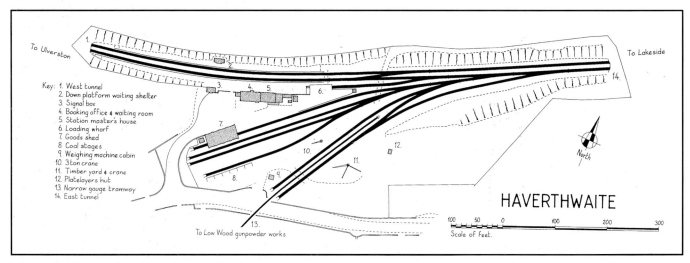

Key: 1. West tunnel
2. Down platform waiting shelter
3. Signal box
4. Booking office & waiting room
5. Station master's house
6. Loading wharf
7. Goods shed
8. Coal stages
9. Weighing machine cabin
10. 3 ton crane
11. Timber yard & crane
12. Platelayers hut
13. Narrow gauge tramway
14. East tunnel

To Ulverston

To Lakeside

To Low Wood gunpowder works

North

HAVERTHWAITE

100 50 0 100 200 300
Scale of feet.

Note the signal beyond the platform, operated from the ground frame at the near end of the waiting shelter by passengers wishing to join trains. Newby Bridge Platform was closed to passenger traffic in 1939, although it was used during the war in connection with the transport of prisoners-of-war to nearby Grizebeck Hall. Reopened by the Lakeside & Haverthwaite Railway in 1973, the platform building had by that time been removed and has since been replaced by a bus-type shelter provided by members of the Lakeside Railway Society, whose intention it is eventually to build a replica of the original waiting shelter. *2390*

Below A passenger train headed by 2-4-2 tank engine No 71 running bunker first is captured on this photograph entering Newby Bridge Platform on its way to Lakeside. In the foreground is a Furness Railway platform seat with the distinctive 'squirrel and grapes' ends. Painted red in urban areas and with alternate red and cream slats on rural stations, the seats usually had the station name painted on the top rail of the back-rest.

As stations closed, or became unstaffed, during the 1960s, the seats were removed and sold to enthusiasts, sometimes for as little as 2s 6d. *4905*

Above This view from a departing steamer shows to advantage the combined station and landing pier at Lakeside. The refreshment pavilion was not always as extensive as it is shown here, originally occupying only some 60 feet in the centre of the wharf. By 1906, however, the accommodation was becoming inadequate to deal with the number of passengers wishing to use it, and managers Spiers & Pond submitted a claim for enlargement of the premises, stating that during the period 1 June to 17 August they had provided 836 breakfasts, 4,305 lunches and 3,551 teas, it being necessary, on several occasions, to set up tables on the landing stage to provide the extra accommodation needed to serve this number of meals. The Railway Company agreed to extend the pavilion by a further 50 feet in the northerly direction in time for the 1907 season. Up to this time, too, the veranda had been open-sided and attention was drawn to the discomfort suffered by diners from smoke and soot due to the close proximity of steamer funnels, with rain also blowing in on wet days. Once again the Railway Company responded, the Board authorising the installation of rolling glass screens at a cost of £150 at its meeting on 30 October 1906.

The steamer still alongside is *Swift*; also, on the right of the picture can be seen the stern and vertical boiler of the barge *Raven*.

There is still an overhead refreshment room at Lakeside station and it still contains some of the original ironwork, but its size has been reduced to approximately that of the 1906 season. *5216*

Above right An interior view of the veranda refreshment pavilion, complete with hanging baskets, under which are posed the members of Bateson's Orchestral Band, a small locally based ensemble that played daily during the summer season for the enjoyment of passengers using the dining room, and occasionally on the lake steamers. Organised by Mr Thomas Bateson of Bowness, who played the cornet, he was supported by his wife, seated in front of him, who played the violin. The harpist was Mr Nightingale from Ely, Mr Booth from Accrington played the flute and Mr Walker of Shipley performed on the double bass. The name of the clarinettist is not known. Started by Mr Bateson's father in 1859, the band

entertained Furness Railway passengers continuously until the end of the 1915 summer season, but the Railway Company Board, at its meeting on 9 May 1916, decided not to continue the practice because of the war, despite protestations from Mr Bateson that none of his players were eligible for military service. *5715*

Below When it was first built, the terminal station of the Lakeside branch, with its yellow bricks and black banding, was considered by many local residents as being too striking, in contrast to the grey Lakeland stone buildings nearby. It was nevertheless, with its steeply roofed tower, an imposing building, officially described as being in an Italianate style of architecture. It had, in addition to its imposing frontage, considerable facilities for the terminus of a branch line aimed primarily at the tourist trade.

The train shed, which had direct access to the steamer landing, housed two platforms served by three roads, and the overhead refreshment veranda gave diners an unrivalled view of Windermere Lake; there was also a goods shed, an engine shed with turntable and a water tower.

Closed when passenger services were withdrawn on the branch on 6 September 1965, this fine building lay derelict until it was declared unsafe because of dry rot, and demolished a few months before acquisition of the site by the Lakeside & Haverthwaite Railway. *4918*

Stank branch

This is part of the Stank branch, which came into operation in 1876 to serve the mines opened at this quaintly named Furness village just to the east of Barrow, after the discovery of iron ore deposits nearby. Mining continued here until 1901 when the mines were closed and the branch line reduced to the short siding seen on this photograph. During building the earthworks were constructed for double track, since at the time there was a proposal, never realised, to build a railway line from Salthouse, through the low Furness villages of Gleaston and Urswick, to rejoin the main line beyond Lindal. In the event only the 2 miles from Salthouse to Stank were ever built.

This photograph would have been taken some time after 1925, as the single-decker bus in the background, on its way to Rampside, is one of five supplied in that year by Guy Motors for use on the coast road route between Barrow and Ulverston. Also in the background can be seen the two rows of terraced sandstone cottages built at Roose between 1873 and 1875 to house Cornish miners, working at Stank, who had moved north in search of employment in the booming Furness mining industry. Known as North and South Rows, the cottages still exist in much the same form as they were built some 120 years ago. *D623*

Piel branch

The line to Rampside and Piel was one of the original sections of the 1846 Furness Railway, leaving the route to Barrow and the iron ore jetties at a junction just south of Roose.

It was built to form a connection with steamer services across Morecambe Bay to Fleetwood, operated by a banker, John Abel Smith, who in 1843 had purchased Roa Island. Here he built a jetty, extending into deep water, for use by his steamers, at the same time joining the island to the mainland by means of an embankment capable of carrying a railway. The Furness Company negotiated rights to operate trains on a line built over the causeway, but by some oversight did not gain access to the steamer pier. Differences between Smith and the Railway Company on this issue led to another pier being built by the Railway Company at Barrow, but this was dependant upon tides, a disadvantage which the Roa Island jetty did not have. The situation became so difficult that the Company entered into negotiations with Smith to lease the embankment, together with Roa Island and its pier, but on 27 December 1852 nature intervened when a great storm severely damaged both pier and causeway. Smith, unwilling to face the high cost of repairs, sold out all his holdings to the Furness Company for the sum of £15,000.

Top right Salthouse Halt, the small platform seen in this picture, was situated on a curve opened in 1873 that left the Barrow-bound line at Salthouse Junction and joined the Rampside section at Parrock Hall Junction.

Built after the First World War, and opened on 22 May 1920, the need for a halt between Barrow and Roose had first been raised by residents of Salthouse as early as 21 January 1909, but the Railway Company's Board deferred the request at the time and finally rejected it on 1 July 1910. The reason for its eventual building on the Piel branch, between Barrow and Rampside, is obscure, but it had its own booking office, which is the small flat-topped wooden hut seen beyond the right-hand crossing gate. The crossing itself admitted vehicular traffic into Barrow's 1917-opened Salthouse Gas Works. *6000*

Middle right The Summer Timetable of 1914 shows five trains in each direction daily, with extra services on Thursdays and Saturdays.

Right Situated at the mainland end of the causeway to Roa Island, the station at Rampside was known originally as Concle station; a nearby inn still carries the name Concle, and it was not renamed Rampside station until 1869. The platform, initially only 192 feet long, was extended to 500 feet in 1911, following delays at the station on Whit Monday of that year when 2,400 passengers were booked, and the short platform made ticket collecting difficult. During the summer of 1920 a special Saturday afternoon train ran taking passengers from Salthouse Halt to Rampside.

Closed to passengers on 6 July 1936, the station and station house, the building on the left of the line, can still be recognised, and traces of the platform can still be found. *6984*

PIEL BRANCH.

DOWN.	WEEK DAYS.								UP.	WEEK DAYS.						
	1	2	3	4	5	6	7			1	2	3	4	5	6	7
		A					*B*				*A*					*B*
	am	am	pm	pm	pm	pm	pm			am	am	pm	pm	pm	pm	pm
Barrow Central...dep	8 5	11 15	12 35	2 30	5 55	8 25	10 45		Piel ....dep	8 23	11 33	1 28	2 48	6 13	8 43	11 3
Rampside .... ,,	8 14	11 24	12 44	2 39	6 4	8 34	10 54		Rampside .... ,,	8 26	11 36	1 31	2 51	6 16	8 46	11 6
Piel ....afr	8 17	11 27	12 47	2 42	6 7	8 37	10 57		Barrow Central...arr	8 35	11 45	1 40	3 0	6 25	8 55	11 15

A—Saturdays only. B—Thursdays and Saturdays only, and on August Bank Holiday.

Below Although situated on Roa Island, the terminal station of the branch was known as Piel station. Steamer services from Piel Pier continued until 1882, at which time they were transferred to the newly constructed steamer berths in Walney Channel, adjacent to the entrance to Ramsden Dock, and, direct boat trains to the island

no longer being needed, the section of line between Roose and Parrock Hall junctions was taken out, thereafter only local services from Barrow being operated. After falling into decay, the pier was finally demolished. As can be seen from the photograph and the plan below, the station was a very simple affair, consisting of a single platform partially covered by a short train shed. A loop line, running outside the shed, allowed engines to run round their trains, and a short siding served the gas works, there being no mains gas on Roa Island until the Salthouse Gas Works was opened in 1917. Movement of engines and trains was controlled from a small signal box on the platform, opened on 15 October 1900, which after closure of the branch became a ground frame box at the north end of Barrow Central station.

The branch closed on 6 July 1936, only a short spur to the gas works being retained, which was extended in 1954 to serve the new Barrow Electricity Generating Station at Roosecote. There is now no trace that the railway ever existed at Roa Island, and of this scene only the Hotel can still be recognised. 6990

Below Map of Piel station, Roa Island. *Mike Faulkner*

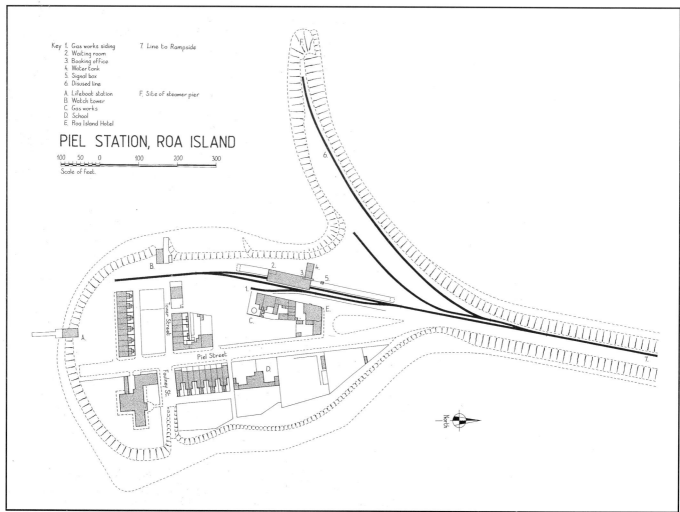

Key 1. Gas works siding
2. Waiting room
3. Booking office
4. Water tank
5. Signal box
6. Disused line

A. Lifeboat station
B. Watch tower
C. Gas works
D. School
E. Roa Island Hotel

7. Line to Rampside

F. Site of steamer pier

PIEL STATION, ROA ISLAND

100 50 0   100   200   300
Scale of feet.

Coniston branch

Broughton was, until 1858, the junction station between the Furness Railway extending northwards from Barrow and the Whitehaven & Furness Junction Railway coming south from Whitehaven. In that year the two systems were linked by the installation of a curve at Foxfield, opened on 1 August, which eliminated the need for through trains to run into Broughton, and the interchange was transferred to a newly built station at Foxfield (see page 47).

The year 1859, however, saw Broughton regain its interchange function with the arrival of the Coniston Railway, a line built principally to transport minerals mined at Coniston, which hitherto had been carried in barges along Coniston Lake for shipping from the small port of Greenodd. The line also had a tourist potential in connection with the steam yacht *Gondola*, which had commenced pleasure sailings on the lake in the same year. The station illustrated here dates from this time, the original station, which would have been situated about on the new trackbed, being demolished to make way for the new line.

The Coniston line, although not initially part of the Furness Railway, was built with that Company's assistance, its directors also served on the Furness Board, and the Furness supplied all motive power and stock used on the railway prior to its amalgamation with the parent company in 1862.

Passenger traffic commenced on the branch on 18 June 1859, but it was to be another year before mineral traffic began. On 8 July 1903 a second offset wooden platform with loop, seen on the left of the photograph, was brought into use at Broughton at a cost of £1,000. This allowed two trains to cross without the need for one of them to be shunted into the goods yard. Later in the same year a further £250 was expended on extensions to the waiting rooms in the main building.

This view of Broughton station, taken from an elevated position to the east, shows the village beyond and Dunnerdale Fell dominant in the background. In the centre a line of Furness Railway wagons stands in front of the goods shed, which itself is partially obscuring the 1903 extensions to the waiting rooms. 5446

Another view of Broughton station, seen from the wooden platform. The signal box, just visible in the background, opened on 31 May 1897 when the branch was re-signalled to comply with the 1889 Regulations of Railways Act. The station closed in 1958 but still exists as two private dwellings. 2532

Right The line from Broughton to Coniston was single track and had two intermediate stations at Woodland and Torver. Woodland, like Broughton, had two platforms with a passing loop, and the station building was also the Post Office. Torver, seen here, had its passing loop taken out in 1897, thereafter having only a single track with a goods shed and goods wharf sited just south of the station, controlled by a ground frame. Woodland and Torver station buildings both still exist as private dwellings, the former preserved almost as it was in Furness Railway days with both platforms and all buildings except the signal box still standing; the latter, too, is still recognisable. The goods shed at Torver is still standing having been renovated and re-roofed following fire damage some years ago. The track bed to the goods wharf and beyond has been incorporated into improvements to the A593 road between Coniston and Broughton. *2756*

Below The Coniston branch and lake steamer services, from the Summer Timetable of 1914.

Coniston Branch and Lake Steamers with Connections.   4

Week Days. / Sundays.

DOWN.

	1	2	3	4	5	6	7	8	9	10	11	12	13	1	2	3	4
	a m	a m	a m	a m	p m		p m	p m	p m			p m	p m	p m	a m	p m	p m
Carnforth ....dep	..	7 0	..	9 50	1215	..	1 25	3 48	4* 0	..	..	6 20			7 35	..	..
Grange .... ”	..	7 25	..	9 55	1231	..	1 50	4 4	4 30	..	..	6 45	Sats. till Sept. 10th		8 0	..	..
Ulverston .... ”	..	7 52	..	1032	1248	..	2 17	4 21	4 57	..	..	7 12			8 21	1 32	6 22
Dalton .... ”	..	8 5	..	1035	1259	..	2 30	4 20	5 10	..	..	7 25			8 40	1 45	6 35
Furness Abbey .... ”	..	8 10	..	1040	1 4	..	2 35	4 25	5 15	..	..	7 30			8 45	1 50	6 40
Barrow {(Dock) ... ”	..	6ʰ45	..	..	12 5	..	..	..	..	..	..	6ʰ10			..	..	6 10
{(Central).. ”	..	8 25	..	1110	1 17	..	2 50	4 45	5 40	..	..	7 45			9 02	30	6 55
Whitehaven, Bransty.. ”	6 40	6 40	..	—	1015	1140	L	1 30	3 35	..	..	5 40	5 40	7e30	8 30	..	5 40	..
Millom .... ”	7 55	7 55	..	9 0	1130	1241		2 45	4 50	..	..	6 55	6 55	9 5	9 45	..	6 55	..
FOXFIELD ....dep	8 14	8 55	9 20	1155	1 40	..	3 20	5 10	6 25	..	7 10	8 15	9 20	10 0	2 57	7 25	..
Broughton.......... ”	8 18	9 0	9 23	1159	1 45	..	3 25	5 13	6 30	..	7 13	8 18	9 23	10 0	3 3	7 28	..
Woodland .... ”	..	9 8	..	12 7	1 53	..	3 30	5 20	6 38	..	..	8 25	9 30	10 10	3	7 35	..
Torver .... ”	..	9 19	..	1214	2 4	..	3 37	5 28	6 49	..	..	8 32	9 38	10 18	3 18	7 43	..
CONISTON ....arr	..	9 25	9 40	1220	2 10	..	3 45	5 35	6 55	..	..	8 40	9 45	10 25	3 25	7 50	..

A Tuesdays, Thursdays and Saturdays only.   **E** Passengers change at Millom.   **F** Daily until September 19th, and afterwards Thursdays and Saturdays only.   **L** Leaves Whitehaven 11-25 a.m. and Millom 12-26 p.m. until July 11th.

For other connections see page 1.

Week Days. / Sundays.

UP.

	1	2	3	4	5	6	7	8	9	10	11	12	13	1	2	3	4
	a m	a m	a m	a m	a m		p m	p m	p m	p m	p m	p m	p m	a m	p m	p m	
CONISTON ....dep	7 30	..	8 40	11 5	1150	..	2 25	4 15	6 0	6 25	..	8*45	..	9 0	3 58	7 0	..
Torver .... ”	7 37	..	8 46	1111	1157	..	2 31	4 22	..	6 31	..	8*51	..	9 6	4 4	7 6	..
Woodland .... ”	7 48	..	8 54	1119	12 8	..	2 39	4 33	..	6 39	..	8*59	..	9 14	4 12	7 14	..
Broughton........... ”	7 56	8 41	9 2	1127	1216	..	2 47	4 41	6 17	6 47	7 52	9* 7	..	9 22	4 20	7 22	..
FOXFIELD ....arr	8 0	8 45	9 5	1130	1220	..	2 50	4 45	6 20	6 50	7 55	9*10	..	9 25	4 23	7 25	..
Millom ....arr	9 3	9 3	..	1148	1 48	..	3 31	5 26	6 35	8 23	8 23	11*38	..	9 41	4 36	7 36	..
Whitehaven, Bransty.. ”	10 7	10 7	..	1 5	2 53	F	4 45	6 17	7 38	9 55	9 55		..	1055	4 50	8 50	..
Barrow {(Central) ... ”	8 35	..	9 40	1210	1 10	F	3 25	5 30	6 42	7 35	..	9*45	..	1025	4 47	7 35	8 55
{(Dock) ... ”	8 45	..	..	..	1 55	H	..	..	6 55	8 25	..		..				..
Furness Abbey .... ”	8 50	..	9 53	1230	1 20	K	3 45	5 50	7 0	7 50	..	10*18	..	1040	4 51	7 50	..
Dalton .... ”	8 55	..	9 58	1235	2 5	..	3 50	5 57	7 5	7 55	..	10*22	..	1045	4 55	7 55	..
Ulverston .... ”	9 8	..	1011	1248	1 37	..	4 3	6 8	7 18	8 8	..	11*23	..	1058	5 8	8 8	..
Grange .... ”	9 37	..	1035	1 12	1 55	F	4 27	6 32	7 35	8 32	..	—	..	5 37	5 37	8 32	..
Carnforth .... ”	10 5	..	11 0	1 40	2 12	..	4 55	7 0	7 52	9 0	..		..	6 5	6 5	9 0	..

A Tuesdays, Thursdays and Saturdays only.   **F** Until July 11th will arrive Barrow 12 55, Ulverston 1-18, Grange 2-42, and Carnforth 1-47 p.m.   **H** Daily until Sept. 19th, and afterwards on Thursdays and Saturdays only.   **K** Commencing July 13th stops to set down from Coniston Branch on informing the Guard at Barrow.   * Saturdays till Sept. 19th only.   † Commencing July 13th.

For other connections see page 1.

CONISTON LAKE STEAMERS.

WEEK DAYS.

DOWN.

	1	2	3	4	5	6	7	8
	E		**E**		**E**	**F**	**G**	**E**
	a m	a m	noon	p m	p m	p m	p m	p m
Waterhead..dep	10 15	11 35	12 0	12 55	1 20	2 45	3 10	4 30
Lake Bank ..arr	10 50	12 10	12 35	1 30	1 55	3 20	3 45	5 5

WEEK DAYS.

UP.

	1	2	3	4	5	6	7	8
	E		**E**		**E**	**F**	**G**	**E**
	a m	p m	p m	p m	p m	p m	p m	p m
Lake Bank ..dep	10 55	12 15	12 40	1 35	2 0	3 25	3 50	5 10
Waterhead ..arr	11 30	12 50	1 15	2 10	2 35	4 0	4 25	5 45

E Till August 31st only.   **F** 30 mts. earlier during September.   **G** 25 mts. later during September.

A Steam Yacht will make the Tour of the Lake on Sundays, leaving Waterhead at 2-0, 4-15 and 5-30 p.m.

Below Coniston station, as seen in this photograph, dates from 1862 and presumably a station of some sort existed before that, the line having been opened three years earlier, although nothing is known of that structure. Designed by Edward Paley, in a 'Swiss chalet' style of architecture that fitted in with the surrounding mountain scenery, the station was enlarged in 1888 and again in about 1896, this time by the addition of another platform, extension of the existing covered platforms and a new signal box.

The three platforms all appear in this photograph of the southern end of the train shed, together with the entrance to an integral goods shed, just visible to the left of the footbridge. Beyond the station at the northern end was a single-track spur, opened in 1860,

which ran to Coppermines Wharf to facilitate the conveyance of copper ore from the mines on the slopes of Coniston Old Man.

Having opened on 18 June 1859, the branch closed to passenger traffic on 6 October 1958. Thereafter a three-times-weekly goods train ran until this too was withdrawn on 30 April 1962, at which time complete closure of the line from Foxfield to Coniston took place. Coniston station was demolished a year or two later after being vandalised. The footbridge, however, has survived and now helps passengers negotiate the tracks at today's 15-inch-gauge railway station at Ravenglass, while part of the frame from the signal box is installed in the box at Park South near Barrow. *6850*

Below In this similar view, a little to the right and looking across the railway in an easterly direction towards the village, the signal box, which was brought from Carnforth F&M junction when Coniston station was enlarged in 1896, can be seen on the left of the picture standing on its local stone plinth with weighbridge and stone-built weigh office. The diverging track beyond the signal box led to a single-road engine shed with turntable, in which the branch engine was stored overnight, in order to be available to operate the early morning passenger service to Foxfield. The shed and turntable fell out of use when British Railways introduced motor-fitted trains, which did not require the engine to be switched to the front of the train for the return journey. There was another, much smaller signal box, housing a ground frame, at the northern end of the station, and this has survived to be installed in a private garden railway in Coniston village. *6851*

5.
FURNESS RAILWAY
LOCOMOTIVES

A group of locomotives stabled outside Barrow shed are being cleaned by volunteers, guarded by troops, during the railway strike of 1919. The engines are mostly 0-6-0 goods engines - Nos 19, 21 and 24 can be identified, while on the right is one of the final batch of 4-4-0 passenger engines built in 1913 and 1914.

Being at the headquarters of the Furness Railway, the shed at Barrow was the largest of the six sheds on the system, the others being at Carnforth and Whitehaven, at the southern and northern ends of the main line respectively, Moor Row, on the jointly owned ex-Whitehaven, Cleator & Egremont system, Lakeside and Coniston, the latter two being only small facilities used mainly for stabling branch-line locomotives overnight.

The shed in the illustration was not the only one to be built at Barrow, the first being on the original line to the iron ore pier and the station at Rabbit Hill. When the Strand station was opened in 1863, a new shed was erected on the site of the original station, which was soon absorbed into the rapidly expanding nearby railway workshops. The final version, seen on the left of this photograph, was built by the Barrow contractors William Gradwell and opened in 1874. Allocated code number 39 by the LMS in 1926, Barrow became 11B under Carnforth in 1935. British Railways altered the number again in 1958 when, at the head of a district including Workington, Oxenholme and Tebay, Barrow became 11A. In May 1960 it was recoded 12E, and in 1963 12C, part of the Carlisle Kingmoor District. Barrow shed finally closed in 1977 when fuelling and stabling facilities were transferred to sidings at Central station. This sandstone structure was demolished shortly afterwards. *7397*

Left Furness Railway locomotive No 3, preserved and exhibited in a glass case on the approach to Barrow Central station when this photograph was taken, was known affectionately by Barrovians as 'Old Coppernob' because of its distinctive copper firebox cover. The 0-4-0 tender engine was one of the Furness Company's four original locomotives, built by Bury, Curtis & Kennedy of Liverpool. She was brought to Barrow by sea, together with her sister, No 4, in time for the opening of the railway in 1846; Nos 1 and 2, which were slightly smaller, arrived earlier, in 1844, to help in the building and commissioning of the line.

This earlier pair did not have very long lives, No 1 being scrapped in 1866, following severe damage by fire at Carnforth, and No 2 being sold to a Northumberland colliery in 1871. Nos 3 and 4, however, continued in service for more than 50 years before the former was withdrawn, in 1899, for preservation, being placed on display in the early 1900s. Number 4 was withdrawn in 1900 for scrapping. *317*

Below left No 3 remained on display in her glass case until 1924 when she was shown at the International Exhibition held at Wembley. She is seen here, with chimney removed, out of her display case and being prepared for the journey to London. After her brief excursion she returned to Barrow where, apart from a short visit to Birmingham in 1938, she was to remain undisturbed until 1941, when on the night of 4-5 May German raiders dropped high explosive bombs on Barrow station entrance and No 1 platform. Not only did these wreck the station, they also demolished 'Coppernob's' glass case and damaged the engine. No 3 was moved to the LMS works at Horwich for safe keeping and later went on display in the Museum of British Transport at Clapham in London. The formation of the National Railway Museum at York in 1975 saw the old engine on the move once more, and this is where she now rests, still bearing her wartime scars. *TP254*

Above right A drawing of No 3, 'Coppernob'.

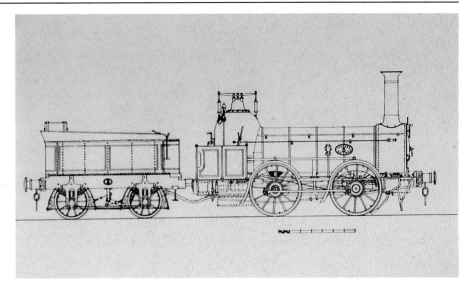

Middle right Although not having the appearance of a Furness Railway locomotive at first sight, Barrow Steelworks industrial saddle tank No 7 began its career as an 0-4-0 tender engine, one of a batch of eight supplied to the Railway Company by builders Sharp, Stewart of Manchester between 1863 and 1866. Numbered 17 to 20 and 25 to 28, these small four-wheeled engines soon became obsolete with the rapid expansion of traffic on the railway during the late 1860s, and in 1870 six (Nos 17, 18, 19, 20, 25 and 26) were sold to the steelworks to be converted to saddle tank engines for internal works use. Nos 27 and 28 remained with the Furness Railway, being employed as dockside shunters until they were scrapped in 1918. *CB12*

Bottom right In 1960 two of the saddle tanks, Nos 7 and 17, formerly FR numbers 18 and 25, were given as static exhibits to special schools, one in Barrow and the other in Ulverston. After 25 years of amusing the children, both engines were taken to the Steamtown Railway Museum at Carnforth, where No 7 is to be restored to its original condition by the Furness Railway Trust, a band of enthusiasts based on the Lakeside & Haverthwaite Railway. The drawing shows how No 7 will look after restoration.

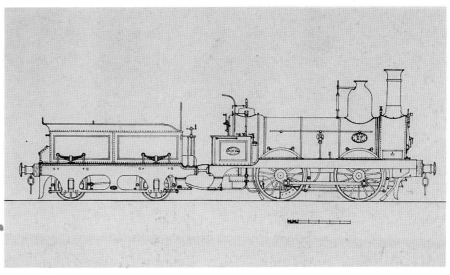

Left Posed at Lakeside station, No 74 was one of a class of seven 2-4-2 tank engines created for branch line duties in 1891 by the rebuilding of 2-4-0 passenger engines in the Furness Railway Company's Barrow workshops. Built by Sharp, Stewart of Manchester, the 2-4-0 tender engines were introduced during the early 1870s to replace smaller 2-2-2 well tank locomotives on main-line passenger services, the well tanks being relegated to lighter duties on the Lakeside and Coniston branches. However, as the tourist traffic expanded rapidly in the late 1880s, the provision of a more powerful class of tank engine became necessary, as the elderly well tanks found ever-increasing difficulty in dealing with heavier branch-line trains. The rebuild, designed by Mr Mason, Locomotive Superintendent at that time, consisted of lengthening the frames to carry a coal bunker, supported by a pair of trailing radial wheels, and adding tanks, with a capacity of 1,000 gallons of water, on either side of the boiler. Of the seven rebuilds only two survived to be taken into LMS ownership in 1923, but No 74 was not one of them, having been scrapped in 1920. *5215*

Left An enlargement from a negative showing the 550-ton Vickers-built submarine HMS *D1* passing through Ramsden Dock. Launched on 16 May 1908, the vessel's departure gives an approximate date to the picture, which is of interest to railway-lovers as it shows an 0-6-0 goods engine shunting on the dockside.

This engine, probably No 64, was one of 18 similar locomotives supplied to the Furness Railway Company by builders Sharp, Stewart in 1871. During the period 1866-82 53 of these engines were put into service to deal with the ever-increasing goods traffic of the time, and they became affectionately known as the 'Sharpies'. A few, vacuum-fitted, were occasionally used on passenger trains, but by the time of the photograph (1908-09) they had largely been relegated to less arduous duties such as shunting, and were superseded on main-line goods trains by more powerful introductions.

Of the original 53 engines, 27 survived to be taken into LMS ownership in 1923, although a number of these were quite different in appearance from the one seen here, having been rebuilt with larger boilers and flat-topped cabs. Some of the rebuilds remained active until 1930, but all of those still in their original form had gone by 1927. The illustrated engine would be similar in appearance to No 115, lost in the Lindal ore sidings subsidence in 1892 (see page 21). No 64 was scrapped in 1918.

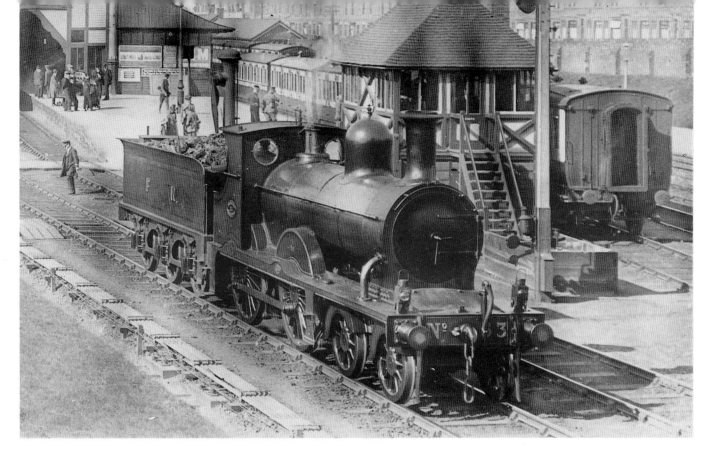

Above Having replaced the small 2-2-2 well tank engines, economical to operate on the relatively light passenger trains of the time, the new Sharp, Stewart 2-4-0 tender engines (see opposite) continued in use for 20 years until they too were proving inadequate to haul trains constantly increasing in weight. More powerful motive power became essential on main-line trains, and this was provided by the introduction, in 1890, of the first of the 4-4-0 passenger locomotives. Five were delivered in that year and a further two in 1891, these being the first bogie locomotives to be used on the Furness Railway.

In 1896 a further six engines of this type were ordered, but of a more powerful class than the 1890-91 introductions, and the illustrated engine was one of these. Numbered 22 when brought into service, this engine became number 33 in 1910 to allow the number 22 to be allocated to a new 0-6-0 tank engine. Another change, in 1920, to No 45 allowed No 33 to be given to a newly introduced 0-6-0 tender engine designed for heavy mineral trains. The date of this picture is thought to be about 1915, and the presence of a number of passengers in military uniform seems to support this. Note the splashers over the wheels of the bogie - these were discontinued on engines ordered after 1900. Allocated number 10138 when taken into LMS ownership in 1923, this engine was scrapped in 1928. *3703*

Above right An immaculate 4-4-0 passenger locomotive, almost certainly No 128, waits with a train in Ramsden Dock station while crew and officials pose for the photographer. One of a batch of four engines ordered from builders Sharp, Stewart in 1901, these were numbered 126 to 129 and, with larger-diameter driving wheels, were more powerful than the 1896 introductions. Note too the absence of splashers

over the bogie wheels. The maker's number for this locomotive was 4718, and at the Grouping in 1923 LMS number 10146 was allocated, a number carried until scrapping in 1930.

The name on the indicator post points to the possibility that this was either a special trip to the Isle of Man, a destination not usually visited by the Furness Railway paddle-steamers, or a boat train running in connection with a Barrow Steam Navigation Company summer service to Douglas. *3470*

Bottom A drawing of 4-4-0 No 128.

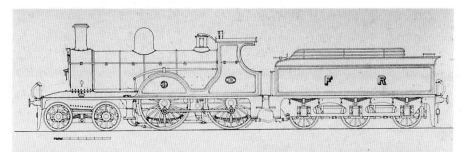

Below Volunteer cleaners pose for the photographer on 0-6-0 goods engine No 24 during the railway strike of 1919. Goods traffic had been in the charge of 0-6-0 tender engines since 1866. Previously 0-4-0 tender engines built variously by Bury, Curtis & Kennedy of Liverpool, Fairbairn & Sons and Sharp, Stewart & Co, both of Manchester, had been used, but by that time it became evident that more powerful traction was needed to handle trains ever increasing in length and weight as mineral traffic expanded. To fulfil this need, 10 six-coupled tender engines were ordered from Sharp, Stewart in 1866, and from that date until 1920 a total of 88 engines of this type was introduced, increasing in power over the years as loads became greater. They were built mostly by Sharp, Stewart, but some were supplied by the North British Company of Glasgow, Kitson of Leeds and Nasmyth, Wilson of Manchester.

No 24, built by the North British Company in 1918, was one of the latest and most powerful of the type and lasted until 1930, when, carrying LMS number 12505, she was scrapped. Her sister engine No 33, her number inherited from a 4-4-0 passenger engine (see previous page) survived until 1957 and, carrying British Railways number 52510, became the last Furness Railway-introduced engine to remain in service, not being scrapped until 1957. *7513*

Below Standing at Ramsden Dock Station signal box is No 102, one of Locomotive Superintendent W. F. Pettigrew's design of 0-6-2 radial tank engines. First introduced in 1898 to supersede ageing locomotives inherited in 1878, when the Whitehaven, Cleator & Egremont line passed into the joint ownership of the Furness and London & North Western companies, these powerful new engines soon became known as the 'Cleator Tanks', after the area in which they originally worked. The 1898 order of three locomotives from Sharp, Stewart was supplemented by a further 10, ordered in 1904, five from Nasmyth Wilson, of which No 102 was one, and five from the North British Locomotive Company.

Although designed for working heavy freight traffic, these engines, when fitted with steam heating apparatus and the vacuum brake, were ideal for economical operating of passenger services, and they appear frequently on photographs performing these duties.

All survived into LMS days, one lasting until 1946, but No 102, carrying LMS number 11029, was scrapped in 1931. The leading passenger coach, a six-compartment brake, was one of eight similar vehicles built during 1901-02, and seated 60 passengers.

Signal boxes of similar design to that at Ramsden Dock Station were built at a number of locations including Dalton station, North Lonsdale crossing, on the Bardsea branch, at St Bees station and at Park South, on the main line north of Barrow. The design dates from the early 1880s, this particular example having opened in June 1885. The latter two are still in operation. *RS2*

Above Until 1920 passenger train operation on the main line had been in the hands of the 4-4-0 passenger engines, the most powerful of which, numbered 130 to 133, had gone into service in 1913 and 1914. It had become necessary, however, on popular trains to use these engines in tandem (see page 31), and a more powerful class of locomotives was needed. The 4-6-4 tank engines that were to fulfil this role were designed during the reign of Mr D. L. Rutherford, who succeeded Mr W. F. Pettigrew as Chief Engineer and Locomotive Superintendent in 1918. Five engines were built by Kitson of Leeds, entering service in 1920. Numbered 115 to 119, these were the final Furness Railway locomotive introductions before absorption into the London, Midland and Scottish Railway in 1923, at which time

they became LMS numbers 11100 to 11104.

The locomotive in this picture, with driver Andrew Riley leaning on the buffer beam, is No 119, and the title of the negative, 'F. R. New Tank Engine', together with its pristine condition, suggests that this could have been the occasion of its inaugural run. Weighing in at 92 tons, with a length of nearly 50 feet, these locomotives quickly became known as 'the Jumbos'. Note the location of the headlamp, high on the boiler. Its position shows that the picture was taken shortly after the class's introduction, as it was soon found that the draught caused by such large engines passing through bridges at speed could extinguish the lamp, and they were soon repositioned lower down the smokebox door, as can be seen on the photograph of number 115 at St Bees (page 61). The position of the lamps in both pictures, at the top of the smokebox door, shows both to have been ordinary passenger trains. *7389*

Below A drawing of one of the 4-6-4 'Jumbos'.

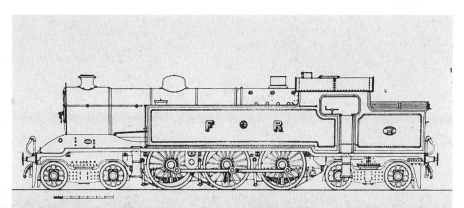

6.
FURNESS RAILWAY VESSELS

Lake steamers

The construction and opening of the Coniston Railway in 1859, while primarily intended for the transportation of minerals, did offer scope for passenger traffic. To further exploit this potential, the steam yacht *Gondola*, financed in part at least by the Furness Railway Company, was launched in October 1859. She was not the first steam-propelled vessel to sail upon Coniston Water; a notice in *Soulby's Ulverston Advertiser* of 12 July 1855, four years before the advent of *Gondola*, announced that a small screw-propelled steamer, *Queen of the Lake*, had been launched at High Nibthwaite, and that on and after 16 July she would ply between Waterhead Inn, Coniston, and High Nibthwaite for the purpose of carrying passengers. Built at Greenodd and believed to have been transported in its completed state overland by teams of horses, the vessel was offered for sale on 16 August 1859, just one month after commencing service, suggesting that the venture might have been proving unprofitable.

This was not to be the case with *Gondola*. Reputedly designed by Mr James Ramsden, and built from riveted Low Moor iron plates by

Jones & Quiggin of Liverpool at a cost of £1,200, she was transported in sections by rail to Coniston, where she was assembled and launched from Pier Cottage slipway, close to Coniston Hall, in October 1859. Originally the fumes from the boiler and two-cylinder engines were exhausted through ducts set in the stern, but these were soon replaced by a raked funnel. The 42-ton vessel, which entered service in 1860, was 84 feet long, 14 ft 2 ins broad, and was registered to carry 200 passengers on her single deck with its large cabin. A gilded figurehead in the form of a serpent, bearing the 'Cavendo Tutus' motto of the Duke of Devonshire, decorated the sweeping bows, she had a clipper stern, tripod mounted mast and luxurious interior appointments; this prompted *The Illustrated London News* to describe her as 'the most elegant little steam vessel yet designed'.

In 1871 *Gondola* was joined by Captain Felix Hamill, at the helm in this photograph, who commanded her for 50 years until his retirement in 1921. During his period of captaincy he is estimated to have made more than 13,000 sailings, during that time causing damage amounting to only 7s 6d.

By 1908, after 45 years service, and with a book value of only £40, it was decided that *Gondola* should be joined, and eventually replaced, by a new, larger steamer named *Lady of the Lake*. Retirement, however, was not to come, and apart from cessation of services during the First World War, both vessels sailed regularly until the commencement of the Second World War in 1939, which once again caused sailings to be suspended, this time never to be resumed under railway ownership.

Sold in 1945 to be converted to a houseboat, *Gondola* sank in 1962, but was refloated and beached in 1965 at the foot of the lake, from where she was rescued by the National Trust in 1978. Fitted with flotation chambers, the derelict vessel was towed to her birthplace at Pier Cottage Slipway, where she was sectioned for transportation to the Vickers Works in Barrow for the rebuilding of her hull and superstructure.

On 25 March 1980 the rebuilt *Gondola* entered the water along the same rails laid down in 1859 for the first launching. Commissioned on 24 June 1980, this lovely steamer now sails daily during the summer season, bringing a nostalgic glimpse of Victorian splendour to the magnificent scenery surrounding Coniston Water. *2298*

Right Intended eventually to replace *Gondola*, although as we have seen she never did so, *Lady of the Lake* was built at Thornycroft's Woolston yard on the south coast at a cost of £5,600. Constructed in sections, she was assembled at Pier House Slipway and launched on Tuesday 26 May 1908. With a total length of 97 ft 6 ins, a breadth of 15 feet and a depth of 6 ft 9 ins, her engines, mounted on either side of a locomotive-type boiler and working at a pressure of 120 lbs per sq in, gave her a speed of 11½ knots. Twin decked, with a spacious, well-ventilated cabin amidships, she was registered to carry 400 passengers, and with her canoe-shaped bow and clipper stern she bore a striking resemblance to the Windermere steam yacht *Tern*.

Never attaining the popularity of *Gondola* with either passengers or crew, it was said that with her engines placed in the stern, she rode with her bows high in the water, which made her difficult to steer in rough and windy weather. Why this should be more noticeable than with *Gondola*, which also had her engines in the stern and was shallow-draughted at the bow, is not clear, but could be attributed to the greater top hamper of 'Lady' being more wind resistant than *Gondola*'s lower freeboard.

There seem to have been very few mishaps involving *Lady of the Lake*, but it is on record that the vessel grounded at Lake Bank in May 1913 owing to a recently appointed engineer named McDowell failing to alter the reversing levers when the captain ordered the vessel to go astern; as a result she continued to go ahead and grounded. The damage was assessed at £28 which included £10 to repair the pier.

Converted to diesel power during LMS ownership, *Lady of the Lake* was withdrawn from service, along with *Gondola*, in 1939 at the outbreak of war and was sold for scrap in 1946. *2344*

Below The Furness Railway Company acquired its interest in the Windermere United Steam Yacht Company at the time when the building of the Lakeside branch was under consideration. Then, three small paddle-steamers, *Firefly*, *Dragonfly* and *Rothay*, were operated on the lake from a small jetty on the River Leven at Newby Bridge. The latter steamer was unique, being double-ended in order that it could operate in and out of the narrow river without having to turn around.

The decision to build a new deep-water steamer jetty combined with a railway station at the foot of the lake, together with the expected influx of passengers brought in by the new line and the trade already generated by the 1847-opened Oxenholme-Windermere railway, made the provision of a new, larger steamer imperative. In consequence a screw-propelled vessel was ordered by the Steamer Company. Built of iron by T. B. Seath of Rutherglen at a cost of £4,000, the new steamer, named *Swan*, was 147 feet long, 17 feet in the beam and had a gross tonnage of 71. Powered by a two-cylinder steam engine developing 20 hp, she was the first screw-propelled steamer to operate on Windermere and the last one to be ordered by the Windermere United Steam Yacht Co. Transported in sections from the builder's yard at Glasgow to be assembled at Lakeside, she was launched on 5 June 1869, four days after the opening of the branch line.

With a capacity for some 450 passengers in two classes with ample cabin accommodation in case of inclement weather, *Swan* was, with her graceful lines, the prototype for all future steamers on the lake. Serving under three different owners - the Windermere United Steam Yacht Company, The Furness Railway Company, and the London, Midland and Scottish Railway Company, *Swan* sailed on until 1938 when she was replaced by a new diesel-powered vessel of the same name, built in steel by Vickers Armstrong Ltd at Barrow, which is still in service. *5324*

Above During a service life spanning 68 years it was inevitable that *Swan*, seen here approaching Lakeside, would experience her share of mishaps, and it is recorded that at 7.15 pm on 27 September 1909 she ran aground in dense fog at Belle Grange, on the western side of the lake, about 2 miles north of the Ferry Hotel. The seven passengers on board at the time were taken by rowing boat to Bowness, and while there were no serious injuries as a result of the accident, the Company had to settle a claim for £10 plus costs of £1 11s 6d from a lady passenger who, it was alleged, was knocked off her feet when the steamer grounded, suffering severe shock. With 66 feet of the forward end of the vessel out of the water it took two days to refloat her.

A further incident, with more serious consequences, happened in Bowness Bay on 22 June 1910, when *Swan* collided with a rowing-boat and two young lady employees of the Old England Hotel were thrown into the water and drowned. The jury at the Coroner's inquest decided that the master and crew of the vessel were not negligent, but added a rider that the design of the vessel was unsatisfactory, suggesting that a bridge be provided on the vessel and a look-out man stationed on the bow when *Swan* was approaching congested parts of the lake. There is, however, no evidence that any action was taken by the Company on either recommendation. *2006*

Below When taken into full ownership by the Furness Railway in 1872, the Windermere steamer fleet consisted of four vessels, the 1869-built screw-propelled *Swan* and the three older paddlers, *Dragonfly*, *Firefly* and *Rothay*, but the latter three were soon replaced by two new steamers, built in steel by the Barrow Shipbuilding Company at a cost of £3,500 each. These were the sister ships *Teal* (illustrated here) and *Cygnet*, which were, to all intents and purposes, identical.

At 52 gross registered tons, they were 100 feet long and 14 feet in breadth; with two-cylinder steam engines, giving a speed of 11½ knots, they could each carry 336 passengers. They entered service in 1879, *Cygnet* being launched on 22 May and *Teal* on 5 June, both ceremonies being performed by Mrs Wadham, wife of Edward Wadham, a Director of the Furness Railway. They were the first steel-hulled vessels to sail on Windermere and were similar in appearance to *Swan*.

Shortly after the First World War, during which *Cygnet* was laid up and *Teal* continued to operate, both steamers failed to comply with Board of Trade requirements and strengthening of the hulls was carried out. Passing into LMS ownership in 1923, *Teal* served her new owners for only three more years before being laid up, to be scrapped in 1927.

A new *Teal* did not appear on the lake for a number of years until a new diesel-engined vessel carrying the name was built in sections by Vickers Armstrongs Ltd of Barrow and launched at Lakeside on 4 July 1936. She is still in service.

In 1924 the LMS replaced the boiler and engine in *Cygnet* by a new internal combustion unit, supplied by the Parsons Motor Company of Southampton, which with a full complement of passengers and a crew of five gave her a speed of 10 knots. *Cygnet* sailed on until 1953 when her then owners, the British Transport Commission, sold her into private ownership. She is believed to have belonged briefly to the Ullswater Steam Navigation Company, but was never transferred to that lake. After changing hands several times, she sank in shallow water on 17 May 1962, where, declared a total constructive loss, she was sold 'as lies' for scrapping. *5207*

Above right *Tern*, with her distinctive canoe-shaped bow embellished with a circular plaque on which is a representation of the bird whose name she carries, was built at a cost of £5,000 by the Essex firm of Forrest & Sons of Wyvenhoe. Launched in 1891, she was, with the exception of her bow, similar in appearance to her sisters *Teal* and *Cygnet*, but was larger than both. With a gross weight of 120 tons, her length of 146 feet and breadth of 18 feet gave her a capacity for 633 passengers, which, together with her crew of five, she carried along at 11 knots. Her machinery, supplied by Westray & Copeland of Barrow, was unusual in that the locomotive-type boiler supplying the steam was mounted beneath the two twin-cylinder engines, which were offset, so that the engine on the port side drove the starboard shaft and vice versa. Two large-diameter propellers turning at the slow rate of 140 revolutions per minute gave the steamer a very smooth, almost gliding motion.

In 1958 *Tern* was rebuilt and converted to diesel power by the fitting of two Gleniffer engines giving a speed of 10½ knots. At the same time her tall, narrow-diameter, bell-mouthed funnel was replaced by a shorter, oval-shaped example, of the type associated with motor ships, and she was converted to a single-class vessel for 608 passengers. A further rebuild, in 1990, saw the original shape of funnel restored and the old vessel returned to something like her original appearance, but alas not steam-propelled. *Tern* is still sailing, possibly the oldest vessel now in operation on Windermere. *2613*

Below Like *Swan*, *Tern* was also involved in some mishaps, and is reported as being in collision with *Swan* at Ambleside at 8.15 pm on Saturday 7 September 1901, which resulted in the sinking of the latter. Salvage proved to be a difficult operation, requiring four pontoons to be brought from Barrow to Greenodd by sea, and then to Lakeside by rail. Upon these were mounted eight winches that lifted *Swan* by means of wire ropes passed round her hull. She was not raised until 17 October, and after temporary repairs the pontoons, with *Swan* suspended between them, were towed by *Tern* to Lakeside, where the salvaged steamer was placed on the slipway for overhaul.

In another incident on 30 August 1910, fire broke out on *Tern* while she was lying at Ambleside Pier, causing damage to the deck, closets and fittings. Repairs are reported to have cost £74. *5202*

EVERY SUNDAY MORNING AND AFTERNOON

FROM

WHIT=SUNDAY TO SEPTEMBER 29th, 1901,

THE NEW S.Y. "SWIFT" WILL RUN IN CONNECTION WITH THE TRAINS.

CHEAP

WEEKLY

TICKETS

ARE ISSUED ON

WINDERMERE

AND

CONISTON LAKES

STEAM YACHT "SWIFT" ON LAKE WINDERMERE.

These Tickets are also issued to Families of from 2 to 5 persons and may be had at the Lake Stations,

AND AT THE

Company's Booking Office, Grasmere.

Above left In pursuance of its policy to promote tourism and develop passenger traffic in the area in which it operated, the Furness Railway Company resolved, in 1899, to obtain a new steam yacht for sailings on Windermere. This was to be built on the same lines as *Tern*, but with 5 feet of additional length and 2 feet of additional beam, the latter to provide space for the considerable bicycle traffic the Company had, by that time, to deal with. However, the new steamer when finally ordered from T. B. Seath of Rutherglen was completely different from the vessels already operating in that she had a through deck from bow to stern with a saloon below, whereas the others all had well decks forward and aft with a saloon amidships. This was a radical departure from the steam yacht concept of the existing steamers, and *Swift*, as the new vessel was named, had a much more workmanlike appearance, resembling closely the steamer *Sir Walter Scott*, built by Seath in the same year to operate on Loch Katrine in Scotland.

Costing some £9,500, with engines supplied by Fisher of Paisley, *Swift* was launched at Lakeside on 25 July 1900, and at a gross tonnage of 203, with a length of 150 feet and breadth of 21 feet, she was much the largest vessel to sail on the lake. Her four-cylinder compound engines, drawing steam from a locomotive boiler, developed 63^1/$_2$ hp and enabled her to carry her complement of 780 passengers at a speed of 15 knots.

Swift remained in service until the outbreak of the Second World War when steamer services were discontinued, but was unable to resume sailings in 1947, as, along with the other coal-fired vessel *Tern*, she was a victim of the coal shortage, and only the oil-burners *Swan*, *Teal* and *Cygnet* were operated.

After conversion to diesel propulsion in 1958, *Swift* was withdrawn from service in 1984 and is now moored at Lakeside, housing a floating museum devoted to the record-breaking Campbell family, although their water speed activities were confined to Lake Coniston. *5692*

Left An advertisement for *Swift* from 1901, the year after she was launched.

Above It is interesting to note that in many instances the lake steamers, as in this picture of *Swift* arriving at Ambleside, are shown to be flying the White Ensign, a flag normally only worn by naval vessels, and in 1910 a Mr Reginald Fletcher of Pinner wrote to the Company objecting to this practice. Mr Aslett replied that as the Admiralty had no jurisdiction over vessels sailing on inland waterways, the Company would take no action on the complaint. Mr Fletcher was not to be put off, however, and made his views known to the Admiralty, with the result that the Furness Railway received a letter, dated 24 September 1913, stating that the wearing of the White Ensign by the Company's steam yachts had been brought to their attention. The letter stated that under normal circumstances the Admiralty only exercised jurisdiction over vessels on tidal waters, but they did not consider it proper for vessels on inland waterways to wear a flag they would not be permitted to fly if they were on the high seas, and they hoped the Furness Railway would discontinue the practice.

The Company's Board, however, decided to ignore the request and it would seem that the practice continued until the Grouping in 1923, when pictures taken in LMS days show the steamers to be flying the Red Ensign. *G11*

Above Designed as a private yacht for Colonel G. J. M. Ridehalgh of Fell Foot, an estate facing Lakeside, *Britannia*, pictured here, was built in sections by T. B. Seath of Rutherglen at a cost of £12,000, an unbelievably high figure in those days for a private yacht. After transport to Lakeside and assembly, *Britannia* was launched on 24 June 1879.

This elegant vessel with her clipper stem, raked masts, raked burnished copper funnel and single-knuckle counter stern, was quite a large craft, with an overall length of 110 feet and a 12-foot beam. Her high-pressure engines, fed with steam by a horizontal tubular boiler working at 120 lbs per sq in, were placed slightly aft of amidships and, developing 100 hp, drove the vessel along at 14 knots.

Heated by steam and lit by gas, generated on board, *Britannia* was taken over by the Furness Railway Company in 1908 as a Directors' yacht and private-hire steamer, for which purpose her capacity of 122 passengers made her eminently suitable. When her purchase was discussed at a Board meeting in London on Friday 22 November 1907, the Directors were informed that the asking price of £600 included 10 tons of lead ballast, two small boats and various articles of equipment. The vessel had previously been offered to the Company, in 1898, for £1,200, and the General Manager went on to say that he had re-negotiated the current price with the

Manchester firm of solicitors handling the sale, who had accepted an offer of £550. Hiring charges for a day of 8 hours varied from 5 to 10 guineas , depending upon the number of passengers.

Britannia is pictured here sailing with a party on board, flying at her foremast her burgee which carried a picture of Britannia, at the main mast the Company house flag of navy blue with a white crown surmounting the Company's initials, and at the stern post the white ensign. The vessel continued to operate until 1915, but her destiny was not decided until 10 May 1918 when the General Manager reported to the Board that *Britannia* had not been, nor was ever likely to be, a source of profit to the Company, and she was put up for sale. As no offers were forthcoming she was broken up and sold for scrap. 5675

Below As befitted her status as a gentleman's private yacht, *Britannia* was luxuriously appointed with, in her panelled saloon, comfortable padded leather seats, a sideboard surmounted by a tall mirror and a dropleaf table. Over the companionway, as might be expected, was a carved figure of Britannia. On deck, as can be seen, the seat ends were elaborately carved in the form of recumbent lions, and the binnacle housing took the form of an eagle with outstretched wings, a furnishing possibly more suitable for holding a bible in a church rather than a compass on a lake steamer. On either

side of the binnacle, engine room telegraphs can be seen, suggesting that this might be the nerve centre for navigating the yacht, yet, as can clearly be seen on the previous illustration, the vessel was steered from a wheel situated in the stern.

After scrapping, the staircase from the aft companionway found its way into the garden of the Station Master's house at Barrow Central, where it was used to give access to a summer house converted from the Furness Railway's old inspection coach. There it remained until destroyed by a German bomb in May 1941. One of the saloon hatches was rescued from the roof of a greenhouse and is now preserved at the Windermere Steamboat Museum. 5685

Right In addition to the passenger fleet, the Furness Railway owned and operated a less glamorous vessel on Windermere, the cargo lighter *Raven*, seen in this photograph moored at Lakeside. Built by T. B. Seath and launched at Lakeside in 1871, the vertical-boilered steamer was used for the transportation of supplies to the communities scattered along the shores of the lake. During the First World War *Raven* was used by the Barrow works of Vickers Sons & Maxim, who fitted rails on the deck and over the bows to enable the laying of an experimental naval mine that the armament firm was developing. Later, in the mid 1950s, *Raven* was used as a platform for the divers who were replacing the wooden piles at Lakeside steamer pier. She is now preserved at the Windermere Steamboat Museum. *5218*

Below The steamer pier at Bowness-on-Windermere was photographed from the lawn of the Belsfield Hotel, once the home of Henry Schneider, founder of Barrow Steelworks, some time after the Grouping of 1923. A steamer, either *Teal* or *Cygnet*, is arriving from Lakeside and a couple of early motor buses are waiting for passengers. The large vehicle on the left is an AEC belonging to Westmorland Motors, which would operate to Ambleside, Grasmere and Keswick, while the smaller Model T Ford owned by Magnet Motors of Windermere would take passengers to nearby Nab Ferry for Hawkshead, or into Windermere town itself.

In Furness Railway days the lake steamers operated throughout the year, connecting with the railway at Lakeside, to provide an essential service for inhabitants. In addition to Bowness and Ambleside, the steamers called if required at landings belonging to hotels at Storrs Hall, Nab Ferry and Low Wood. Winter services were discontinued, however, after the 1919-20 season, in view of mounting deficits from operating the service, but to alleviate hardship to lakeside dwellers who relied upon the steamers as a vital transport link, the Furness Railway Company negotiated with the Lake District Road Traffic Company and the British Automobile Traction Company for a substitute road service to be initiated, at the same time considering the acquisition of its own motor bus to work the route. This is in fact just what happened, and a Ford motor omnibus was bought at a cost of £370, with an option to resell for £200 after six months. The new vehicle was housed in a garage in Ulverston Goods Yard, erected in 1920 especially for this purpose, and the Furness Railway thus joined other pre-Grouping railway companies such as the LNWR and GWR in operating buses, as well as trains, for transporting passengers. During the winters of 1920-21 and 1921-22 the bus lost amounts of £510 and £260 respectively, which nevertheless compared favourably with a loss of £1,063 from steamer working during the winter of 1919-20. The greatly reduced cost of operating motor transport was already making itself felt. *9888*

Cross-bay steamers

Above In order to transport holidaymakers from the Fylde coast across Morecambe Bay as part of its programme to encourage tourist traffic, the Furness Railway Company ordered a new paddle-steamer from John Scott & Co of Glasgow, which was launched from their Kinghorn Yard in July 1900. Named *Lady Evelyn* after the wife of Mr Victor Cavendish, a Furness Railway Company Director, she was 170 feet long, 24 feet broad, 8 feet in depth, and had a gross weight of 295 tons. With a round stern, single deck and twin masts, she had a speed of 13 knots. Entering service on 26 May 1901, in her inaugural year she carried 29,165 passengers with receipts of £1,798. Her appearance then was very different to that shown in this photograph, for in 1903 it was realised that she was too small to deal with the available traffic, and in order to increase her pas-senger-carrying capacity she was taken into the Vickers yard to be lengthened by 30 feet, at a cost of £6,500.

Re-registered on 17 August 1904, her new length was 200 feet; she now had two decks, an elliptical stern, but only one mast. She is seen here steaming in Walney Channel, with only her crew on board. *Lady Evelyn* remained in service until the end of August 1914, being withdrawn shortly after the declaration of war. Requisitioned by the Admiralty in 1916, she returned to Barrow after two years of service with the Royal Navy to be sold to W. H. Tucker of Cardiff, entering service in the Bristol Channel with that Company on 14 June 1919. There she remained until 1921, at which time Tuckers were taken over by P. & A. Campbell, and *Lady Evelyn*, renamed *Brighton Belle* on 15 May 1923, moved to the South Coast where she stayed until the outbreak of war in 1939. In October of that year she was once again called up for war service and, fitted out as a minesweeper, served until 28 May 1940 when, taking part in the evacuation of the British Expeditionary Force from Dunkirk, she struck a wreck in the English Channel and sank, 39 years almost to the day after first entering service with the Furness Railway.

Lady Evelyn was not the first steamer owned by the Furness Railway Company to sail across Morecambe Bay - that distinction goes to the small screw-propelled steamer *Helvellyn*, which had sailed, under the name *Windermere*, between Liverpool and Ulverston since 1835. She was purchased by the Furness Railway in 1847, and under her new name operated a service between Barrow and Fleetwood following a series of disagreements between the Company and John Abel Smith, owner of Piel Pier (see page 70). *944*

Left Gleaming connecting rods and massive crankshafts driving the paddle-wheels dom-inate this photograph taken in *Lady Evelyn*'s engine room, with the dials of the engine room telegraphs above. The twin-cylinder compound engines built by the vessel's builders, John Scott & Co of Glasgow, with their 22 in x 48 in cylinders and 54-inch stroke developing 141 hp, gave her a speed of 13 knots. The engineer and his three assistants pose proudly in the background. *547*

Above *Lady Margaret*, seen here tied up at Ramsden Dock landing stage, was purchased in May 1903 to supplement *Lady Evelyn* after that steamer, in her original form, had been unable, single-handed, to deal with the volume of passenger traffic between Barrow and Fleetwood during the 1902 season. Indeed, on several occasions the tug *Furness* had been required to help out (see page 96).

Lady Margaret, built in the Dumbarton yard of A. McMillan & Sons to the order of the Lady Margaret Steam Ship Company, was launched on 12 June 1895 and entered service with the Furness Company on 30 May 1903. She was 210 feet long, 25 feet broad,

8.7 feet in depth, weighed 369 tons and had a speed of 17 knots. She had sailed under several owners, including P. & A. Campbell, before she joined the Furness fleet, where she stayed for five seasons before being sold on to the Admiralty for the sum of £14,000. The reason for her sale is not clear; she certainly was not worn out as her new owners used her as a tender for a further 15 years before selling her for breaking up in 1923, so perhaps the price offered was just too good to refuse. *299*

Below Advertisement from *The English Lakes Guide* of 1907.

Below Following the sale of *Lady Margaret*, a replacement vessel was required for the 1908 season and a charter was considered until a new steamer could be purchased. However, the charter terms required by owners of suitable ships were prohibitive, and in April 1908 the paddle-steamer *Philomel* was purchased through James Little & Co from the General Steam Navigation Company of London at a cost of £5,250. Built in 1889 by John Scott & Co of Kirkcaldy, she was one of a fleet of vessels all named after birds ('philomel' is another name for the nightingale). Operating out of London on routes to the East Anglian and Kentish coasts, she was 236 feet in length, 27 feet in breadth, 9.5 feet in depth and was designed to sail at 17 knots. Although new to the Furness Railway, *Philomel* was 19 years old when the Company bought her, and it was not until 1 June 1908, after pre-service restoration work costing £722 had been carried out, that she entered service.

Philomel, soon to be nicknamed 'Full-o'-smell', proved to be a poor investment, and after only two seasons on the Fleetwood run she was found to need a new boiler which, with fitting and other necessary alterations, would cost an estimated £5,000. The vessel's boiler was of an unusual vertical design, with four firebox doors for feeding coal to the fire, and this may have accounted for the high cost of replacement, which when added to the purchase price, plus the post-delivery expenditure, made repair an unacceptable proposition; it was consequently decided to obtain a replacement vessel for the 1910 season. Attempts to sell *Philomel* were unsuccessful because of the state of her boiler, and the Furness Company was left with the vessel on its hands for another three years before selling her for scrap in 1913. *721*

Below left Withdrawal of *Philomel* at the end of the 1909 season left the Furness Railway Company once again without a second steamer to operate its cross-bay services in 1910. However, in November 1909 Mr Aslett reported to the Board that the Barry Railway Company was prepared to sell its five-year-old paddle-steamer *Devonia* for £22,750, the Furness Company to collect from Barry Docks. Built in 1905 at a cost of £29,000, *Devonia* had a No 3 certificate for 1,015 passengers, a speed of 19 knots, and was just what the Furness Railway was looking for. An offer for the required £22,750 was made subject to a favourable report on hull, engines and boiler, but Mr Pettigrew's report on the machinery was unsatisfactory and the offer was withdrawn.

The year 1910 came with no new steamer available, so the Board authorised repairs to the boiler and hull of *Philomel*, should a replacement not be found in time, but almost at the last minute, in April 1910, *Devonia*'s sister ship *Gwalia* was purchased from the Barry Railway Company at a cost of £22,750. Built by John Brown & Co of Clydebank, she was launched on 24 February 1905, was 245 feet long, 29 feet broad, 9.7 feet in depth and had a speed of 17 knots. The change of name from *Gwalia*, an ancient name for Wales, quite unsuitable for a vessel sailing in Furness

Railway colours, to *Lady Moyra*, after the wife of the Company Director Lord Richard Cavendish, was registered on 26 May 1910. In her new livery of blue hull, with white upperworks and yellow funnels, *Lady Moyra* entered service at the beginning of June 1910.

Another ship was purchased from the Barry Railway in June 1910, not this time an addition to the passenger fleet, but a model of *Gwalia* costing £50, which, mounted on a wheeled carriage, was used on the streets of Blackpool to advertise the Company's tours and also as an exhibit in hospital parades in Barrow.

Together with *Lady Evelyn*, and aided if required by the paddle-tug *Walney*, *Lady Moyra* sailed under Furness colours until 30 September 1914, when the Barrow to Fleetwood service ended at the beginning of the war, never to be restarted in earnest. Requisitioned by the Admiralty in 1915, *Lady Moyra* followed *Lady Evelyn* into the Bristol Channel with W. H. Tucker & Co in 1919, to be later renamed *Brighton Queen* by P. & A. Campbell. Transferred to services out of Brighton by her new owners, she was converted once more to a minesweeper in 1939, and sank after being bombed on 31 May 1940 while taking part in Operation Dynamo, the evacuation of the British Expeditionary Force from Dunkirk. *1665*

Tugs

The 180-ton paddle-tug *Lismore* was built for the Furness Railway Company by the Barrow Shipbuilding Company, and was launched on 2 February 1874. The single-decked vessel, powered by two 100 hp diagonal engines with 36-inch diameter cylinders and 5-feet stroke made in Barrow by the shipbuilder, was registered at Barrow

on 6 November 1874. She remained at her home port until sold to William Cooper and Sons Ltd, Dredgers, Steamships and Barge Owners, of Widnes in Lancashire, on 3 November 1920, and was re-registered at the port of Liverpool on 5 December 1922.

This photograph, taken from the tug *Furness*, shows *Lismore* in Walney Channel helping to tow the Brazilian battleship *Sao Paulo* to the fitting-out berth in Buccleuch Dock, after her launch at the Vickers shipyard on 20 April 1909. *703*

Above The twin-screw tug *Furness* is seen here towing part of the floating dock *Alphonso Perra*, built for the Brazilian Government and launched in three sections during June 1910. Built for the Furness Company by J. P. Rennoldson & Co at South Shields in 1898, the 225-ton single-decked tug, registered at Barrow on 5 September 1898, was 128 feet long, 24 feet broad with a depth of 11 feet. Her two Rennoldson-built four-cylinder engines drew steam from boilers manufactured by J. T. Eltringham of South Shields working at 110 lbs per sq in, which, driving twin screws, gave the tug a speed of 12 knots. Used occasionally to help the paddle-steamers on the cross-bay services at busy times, *Furness* remained at Barrow throughout her life. Passing into LMS ownership in 1923, her registry was cancelled on 14 November 1936 and she was scrapped in 1937. *939*

Below The tug *Cartmel*, photographed at work towing the battleship HMS *Princess Royal* in Walney Channel, was built for the Furness Railway Company at Barrow by Vickers Sons & Maxim Ltd, who owned the shipyard at that time.

Sponsored by Miss Turner, daughter of a Furness Railway Director, she was launched on 13 August 1907, and was 125 feet long, 25 feet wide and 13 feet deep, with a gross tonnage of 304. Steam engines developing 1,025 hp, driving twin shafts, gave her a speed of 11½ knots, and together with the tug *Furness* she was a familiar sight in and around Barrow Docks between the wars. Unlike *Furness*, however, she did not spend her entire life at Barrow, being sold by the LMS to Redhead & Sons (Tugs) Ltd of Newcastle in 1934, who in turn sold her on to Leith Salvage & Towing Company Ltd. *1584*

An action-filled scene photographed in December 1920 as the Cunard liner *Scythia*, launched at the Vickers shipyard on 23 March 1920, is being towed out of Buccleuch Dock for completion in France, following a strike of Barrow joiners that had caused work on her to be stopped. Assisting in the movement are three Furness Railway tugs, the twin-funnelled *Furness* and *Cartmel* at the liner's bow, with the paddle-tug *Walney* (see overleaf) hurrying along the dock on the right. 1975

Above The paddle-tug *Walney*, captured in this photograph in her passenger-carrying role, was the second tug of that name to be owned by the Furness Railway. The first, 146 feet long, 20 feet broad and 10 feet deep, was built at Greenock in 1868, and registered at Barrow on 21 May 1868. She was sold to C. C. Duncan, tug-boat owner of Middlesbrough, and her registry was transferred to that port on 2 April 1897, her replacement in the Furness fleet of tugs being *Furness*.

The illustrated vessel was designated a tender, that is a tug with passenger accommodation, and she was built by Rennoldson of South Shields for the Furness Company, coming to Barrow in 1904. During her time with the Railway Company, *Walney* was used frequently to help out on cross-bay passenger services. With a length of 120 feet, breadth over paddles of 35 feet and a depth of 8½ feet, it is on record that she assisted in refloating the destroyer *Legion*, which went aground off Piel on 7 February 1916.

Walney remained in Barrow for 26 years, passing into LMS ownership in 1923, before being transferred by her new owners to Scotland in 1930, where she worked in the ports of Ayr and Troon.

In 1950 *Walney* passed into the hands of the Docks & Inland Waterways Executive, who scrapped her two years later in 1952. *1671*

Below This smart little launch, named *Scout*, was photographed while engaged on light towing duties in Buccleuch Dock in the days when the western dockside was used for landing timber, and before it was taken over by Vickers in 1907 to become the fitting-out berth for the large naval vessels under construction at that time.

Little is known about *Scout*, although her appearance suggests that she might also have been used as a tender, and the only official reference to the vessel that can be found is in a minute of a Board Meeting held on 14 June 1916 referring to payments made by the Admiralty for hire of the Furness Railway Company's vessels. A sum of £4,601 had been received, representing a hire charge of £8 per day for use of either *Furness* or *Cartmel*, depending upon which tug was available, and £1 per day for use of the steam launch *Scout*. How things have changed - it is unlikely at the present time that even a rowing-boat could be hired for a day at those figures! *771*

Dredgers and hoppers

Above Bucket dredger No 4 at work in Buccleuch Dock, probably deepening the dock adjacent to the Vickers fitting-out wharf to accommodate the large naval vessels being built in the shipyard. Little is known of the Railway Company's dredgers, and the only record that has been found refers to a steam dredger, No 1, being launched at the yard of the Barrow Shipbuilding Company for the Furness Railway on 26 October 1874, the vessel being 163 feet long, 27 feet broad with steam engines of 300 hp. The engines were used purely to drive the bucket chain, and the dredger itself, having no means of propulsion, had to be moved to its working area by a tug.

The persistent problem of silting of the approach channel in the narrows between Roa Island and Piel Island required constant dredging, and while some of this work was sub-contracted to spe-cialist dredging companies, the Railway Company needed its own vessels to keep the docks and entrances free from silt. Indeed, the cost of this work was one of the reasons that Barrow never became the major port envisaged by Sir James Ramsden when he first began the building of the docks in the mid-1860s. *1035*

Below Steam hopper barges were required to carry the silt lifted by the dredgers out into the deep waters for discharging, and here hopper No 3 is receiving spoil from dredger No 4 at the northern end of Buccleuch Dock. Built by Vickers Sons & Maxim Ltd for the Furness Railway Company, No 3 was launched on 1 August 1907 and completed in October of that year.

Weighing 424 gross tons, No 3 was 150 feet long, 29 feet broad and 11 feet deep, with two-cylinder compound engines giving her a speed of 9¼ knots. She passed into LMS ownership in 1923, and at the nationalisation of the railways in 1948 was taken over by the British Transport Commission. No 3 was scrapped in 1949. *1033*

Ferries

Above Until the construction of Devonshire and Buccleuch Docks in the waterway between Barrow village and Barrow Island during the mid-1860s, access to Walney Island had, from very early times, been by means of a number of fords. However, the dredging of a deep-water channel between Barrow Island and Walney, necessary to allow shipping to enter the docks at their northern end, had effectively destroyed the traditional crossing places and complaints made to the Railway Company by the inhabitants of Walney eventually resulted in the installation of a chain-operated steam ferry. Launched from a slipway of the Barrow Shipbuilding Company in 1878, the ferry, seen here leaving the Barrow side of the channel, was, because of its design, known locally as the box ferry.

The narrow three-storeyed building on the right of the ferry booking office and entrance was Ivy Cottage, the ferry-keeper's lodge. *230*

Below The box ferry continued to operate until the establishment, in 1900, of Vickerstown, a housing community built by the Barrow shipbuilders to house its expanding workforce, at which time the provision of a larger ferry became a necessity. This was ordered in 1901 from the local shipyard, and was launched on 15 March 1902, entering service on 21 November of that year. The photograph shows this ferry leaving Barrow Island on its way to Walney on the other side of the Channel, and it is on record that during the year 1903 56,970 passengers were carried, with receipts of £133. Until May 1903 the last run of the ferry was 11.30 pm from Barrow and 11.45 pm from Walney, but, following an application from the Isle of Walney Estate Company, sailings were extended by half an hour in each direction. Both ferries remained at Barrow, although only the later one was normally in use, until they were made redundant by the building of Walney Bridge, an undertaking strongly opposed by the Railway.

The new bridge was opened on 30 July 1908 by the Mayoress of Barrow, Mrs T. F. Butler. Shortly after this both ferries were taken to Southampton, the 1878 vessel to become a houseboat and the 1902 vessel to resume her passenger-carrying activities as a ferry across the River Itchen. It is believed that both ferries survived until the 1970s. *230A*

7.
TOURS AND EXCURSIONS

It was under the management of Alfred Aslett that the encouragement of passenger and tourist traffic really gathered momentum. Born and educated at York, Mr Aslett followed his father into service with the Great Northern Railway on 1 May 1863, where he spent 26 years working at Nottingham and King's Cross. This was followed by some 10 years as General Manager with the Eastern & Midlands Railway (later incorporated into the Midland & Great Northern Company) in Norfolk, before being appointed to a similar post with the Cambrian Railways in 1891.

He succeeded Sir James Ramsden as General Manager of the Furness Railway in 1895, at a time when the Company was carrying out improvements to the passenger-carrying side of its business in order to offset reduced income from freight traffic; in 1897 he took on the additional duties of Secretary. Under Mr Aslett's management the passenger initiative was accelerated, and existing tourist facilities expanded until a programme of 20 tours was offered, visiting most of the beauty spots of the Lake District utilising horse-drawn transport to reach places not served by the Railway or its fleet of lake steamers.

The Company's passenger-carrying stock was already being upgraded in order to comply with the continuous brake requirement of the Regulation of Railways Act of 1889, and Mr Aslett gave priority to the programme, introducing well-appointed bogie stock.

Mr Aslett is seen here, with his dog, in front of one of the decorated trams that made the inaugural run to open the new service from Barrow town centre to Bigger Bank on Walney Island on 4 August 1911.
3353

Romney's Early Home

Right George Romney, the eminent portrait artist, was born the son of a cabinet-maker at Beckside, Dalton-in-Furness, on 15 December 1734, and in 1742 the family moved to a cottage at High Cocken, some two miles from Barrow, where they lived until 1755. In 1909 the Furness Railway Company bought and restored the cottage in which Romney had spent his youth and early manhood, turning it into a tourist attraction. In his father's former workshop they created a museum, in which were displayed a number of the artist's portraits in the form of engravings and photogravures. The cottage and museum, which opened on 1 July 1909, were included in the itinerary of a tour that also visited Furness Abbey, Barrow Island and Walney, the latter made possible by the recently opened bridge over Walney Channel replacing the awkward railway-owned steam ferry.

A proposal to erect a refreshment pavilion adjacent to the museum at a cost of £400 was deferred until the amount of interest generated by the museum, admission to which was by production of a rail ticket, became known.

The photograph shows the restored cottage standing high above the village of Ormsgill, with two Furness Railway guides in attendance. In the background, to the right of the flagpole, can be seen the buildings and chimney of the Furness Soap & Candle Works. *2472*

VI.

George Romney's Home
BARROW-IN-FURNESS. (1742-1755)

Distance—1½ miles from Furness Abbey Station and Hotel ; 1¾ miles from Barrow Central Station.

The Grounds surrounding the "Home" have been considerably extended   Open all the year round.

George Romney's Home from 1742 to 1755 has been restored, and a Museum built on the site of the old Workshop.

The Charge for admission to the " Home " and Grounds is 1d. each person, holders of Railway Tickets being admitted free.

SUPERB VIEWS of the Duddon Estuary, Black Combe, Walney Channel and Walney Island, from the Pleasure Grounds surrounding the Home.

RAIL AND COACH TOUR No. 20
including
GEORGE ROMNEY'S HOME, Furness Abbey, Walney Bridge and Walney Island.
IN OPERATION from Whitsuntide to September 30th.

MORNING TOUR.—Coach leaves Barrow Central for George Romney's Home, High Cocken, thence to Furness Abbey, via Sowerby Woods.

AFTERNOON TOUR. —Coach leaves Furness Abbey Station, via Sowerby Woods to George Romney's Home, thence through the principal Streets of Barrow, over the High Level Bridge, from which views of Barrow Docks and Messrs. Vickers' Works are obtained, over the new Bridge spanning Walney Channel, returning to Barrow Central Station.

(Subject to alteration during the Season. See special announcements)

NEW TEA PAVILION WITHIN THE GROUNDS. REFRESHMENTS AT POPULAR CHARGES.

Below right Such was the public interest in Romney's Cottage and museum that, as the caretaker's records show, 1,309 visitors, travelling from 188 different towns and cities, had presented railway tickets to gain admittance. This was sufficient for the Board to agree, at their meeting on 7 April 1910, that the tea pavilion should be constructed forthwith at a cost of £350, with a further £150 allocated for the provision of fences, footpaths and seats. Also in 1910 it was decided that in view of the interest shown by locals, residents and their families who did not hold a railway ticket would be admitted on a payment of 1d.

Perched on the brink of Hawcoat Quarry from whence had come the sandstone used in the building of Barrow's docks, the pavilion gave extensive views to the Lake District, Walney Island and the Irish Sea beyond. Unfortunately, as can be seen in this photograph, the view on one side included Barrow Iron & Steel Works with its slag bank, the Soap & Candle Works and a brickworks.

In conjunction with the cottage and museum venture, two sets of postcards were published depicting some of Romney's works. Unlike other official postcards marketed by the Company at the time, which were supplied by Raphael Tuck, these two series of Romney paintings were produced by James Atkinson of Ulverston and contained several pictures of Emma Hart, better known as Lady Hamilton, mistress of Lord Nelson. *2762*

17

Tour No. 15.   Six Lakes Circular Tour.

INCLUDING

Windermere, Rydal, Grasmere, Thirlmere, Derwentwater, and - - - Ullswater. - - -

Through Tickets available for return any day within a week, with break of journey at any station on the Circle.

Via KESWICK
ON OUTWARD JOURNEY. Passengers travel via Windermere (Lake Side) and Ambleside, thence per Taylor's Coach to Keswick, Keswick to Penrith by Rail, Penrith to Pooley Bridge by Motor Car, Pooley Bridge to Patterdale (Ullswater) by Steamer, and Taylor's Coach from Patterdale to Ambleside.

Via ULLSWATER
ON OUTWARD JOURNEY. Passengers travel via Lake Side, Windermere, and Ambleside, thence per Taylor's Coach to Ullswater, thence from Patterdale to Pooley Bridge by Steamer; Pooley Bridge to Penrith by Motor Car. Penrith to Keswick by Rail, and Taylor's Coach from Keswick to Ambleside.

ULLSWATER (STYBARROW CRAG).

MAP OF TOUR No. 15

OUTWARD JOURNEY—

				a.m.	a.m.	a.m.
Whitehaven { Bransty	...	dep.	—	6 40	10 15	
{ Corkickle	...	,,	—	6 44	10 19	
St. Bees ...	...	,,	—	6 53	10 23	
Seascale ...	...	,,	—	7 14	10 49	
Millom ...	...	,,	—	7 55	11 30	
Askam ...	...	,,	—	8 21	11 56	
Barrow ...	...	,,	—	8 40	12 20	
Furness Abbey	...	,,	—	8 50	12 30	
Dalton ...	...	,,	—	8 55	12 35	
Carnforth	...	,,	—	8 15	12 10	
Silverdale	...	,,	—	8 24	12 19	
Arnside	...	,,	—	8 30	12 26	
Grange	...	,,	—	8 40	12 35	
Kents Bank	...	,,	—	8 45	12 40	
Cark	...	,,	—	8 51	12 46	
Ulverston	...	,,	—	9 10	1 5	
Greenodd	...	,,	—	9 19	1 14	
Haverthwaite	...	,,	—	9 26	1 21	
Lake Side (Steamer) ...	...	,,	8 35	9 45	1 40	
Ambleside (Steamer)...	...	arr.	9 45	10 55	2 50	
Ambleside (Coach)	dep.	10 0				
Ullswater { (Coach)	arr.	12 15	—	—		
(Patterdale) { (Steamer)	dep.	1 45	3 55	—		
Ullswater { (Stmr.)	arr.	2 35	4 45	—		
(Pooley Bdge.) { (Motor)	dep.	2 40	4 50	—		
Penrith (Motor) ...	arr.	3 20	5 40	—		
Ambleside	...	dep.	10 0	11c 0	3 10	
Keswick { (Coach)	...	arr.	12 45	1c 45	6 0	
{ (Train)	...	dep.	3 55	6 29	7 55	
Penrith (Train)	...	arr.	4 40	7 14	8 50	

FARES.

	1	3
	34/-	22/-
	33/9	22/-
	32/6	21/6
	30/3	20/3
	24/9	17/6
	21/9	16/-
	22/3	16/3
	21/3	15/9
	20/9	15/6
	24/-	16/9
	23/-	16/6
	22/3	16/3
	21/3	15/9
	20/9	15/6
	20/-	15/-
	19/3	14/9
	18/-	14/3
	17/3	13/9

Via ULLSWATER. RETURN FROM PENRITH BY TRAIN.

Via KESWICK. RETURN FROM PENRITH BY COACH.

RETURN JOURNEY—

					p.m.	a.m.	p.m.
Penrith (Train) ...	...	...	dep.	5 45	7 30	3 15
{ (Train) ...	...	...	arr.	6 23	8 14	3 54
Keswick					a.m.	p.m.
{ (Coach) ...	...	dep.		9 50	4 0
Ambleside (Coach)	...	arr.		1 0	7 0
Penrith (Motor) ...	...	dep.		9 0	2 8
Ullswater { (Motor)	...	arr.		9 30	2 45
(Pooley Bridge) { (Steamer) ...		dep.		9 35	2 50
Ullswater { (Steamer) ...		arr.		10 20	3 40
(Patterdale) { (Coach) ...		dep.		—	4 0
Ambleside (Coach) ...	...	arr.		6E	6 30
Ambleside (Steamer) ...	...	dep.		2 40	
Lake Side ...	...	,,		4 0	
Haverthwaite ...	...	arr.		4 8	
Greenodd ...	...	,,		4 15	
Ulverston ...	...	,,		4 25	
Cark ...	...	,,		6 22	
Kents Bank ...	...	,,		6 23	
Grange ...	...	,,		6 32	
Arnside ...	...	,,		6 44	
Silverdale ...	...	,,		6 51	
Carnforth ...	...	,,		5 2	
Dalton ...	...	,,		5 10	
Furness Abbey ...	...	,,		5 15	
Barrow ...	...	,,		4 52	
Askam ...	...	,,		5 58	
Millom ...	...	,,		5 25	
Seascale ...	...	,,		5 58	
St. Bees ...	...	,,		6 17	
Whitehaven ...	...	,,		6 30	

Passengers return from Ambleside following day or any day within the week.

Passengers travelling via Keswick on the outward journey must give twelve hours' notice to Mr. Taylor, Coach Proprietor, Ambleside, as to date of return from Ullswater.   C—Tuesdays, Thursdays, and Saturdays only, and when not less than six passengers.   E—Via Dalton.

An **excellent Luncheon** will be supplied at the "Waterhead," "Queen's," or "Salutation" Hotels, at 2/- per head, and **Tea** (including Cakes, Jam, &c.) at 9d. per head to Passengers by this Tour.

For Coach Tours from Keswick, see page 14.

In common with other railways that promoted tourist traffic, the Furness Railway Company produced a great deal of publicity material to lure the public on to its trains. Tourist guides extolling the beauties of the Lake District, together with lists of accommodation available, were published and regularly updated. The Company's programme of some 20 tours throughout Lakeland, with itineraries, timetables, fares and maps, were detailed in a free guide (*above right*).

The tours varied widely in length and complexity, some being simple affairs completed in half a day, while others, such as Tour No 15

'Six Lakes Circular Tour' illustrated here, which visited the lakes of Windermere, Rydal, Grasmere, Thirlmere, Derwentwater and Ullswater, involved the tourist in rail travel over the Cockermouth, Keswick & Penrith Railway and steamer travel in the steam yachts of the Ullswater Navigation & Transit Company. Unless it started very early in the morning, this tour could not be completed in a single day, and tourists had to spend one night in either Keswick or Penrith. Many of the tours were circular, could be joined at any point on the tour and did not need to be completed in the same day.

20

COACH & STEAM YACHT
Tours through Lakeland

DAILY,

From WHIT-MONDAY, MAY 27th, to SEPTEMBER 30th, 1901.

No. 1. Outer Circular Tour, embracing Windermere Lake, Furness Abbey, and Coniston.

No. 2. Inner Circular Tour, embracing Furness Abbey, Coniston Lake (Gondola), and Crake Valley.

No. 3. Grange and Windermere Circular Tour, embracing Grange, Kendal, and Windermere Lake.

No. 4. Middle Circular Tour, embracing Windermere Lake, the Crake Valley, and Coniston Lake.

No. 5. Red Bank and Grasmere Tour, *via* Ambleside and Skelwith Force.

No. 6. Thirlmere, Grasmere, and Windermere Tour, *via* Ambleside, Clappersgate, and Red Bank.

No. 7. The Four Lakes Circular Tour, viz.:—Coniston, Grasmere, Rydal, and Windermere.

No. 8. Coniston to Coniston Tour, *via* Red Bank, Grasmere, and Ambleside.

No. 9. Tarn Hows Tour, *via* Ambleside and Coniston, returning *via* Tilberthwaite and Elterwater.

No. 10. Round the Langdales and Dungeon Ghyll Tour, *via* Ambleside, Colwith Force, Grasmere, and Rydal.

No. 11. Ullswater Tour, *via* Ambleside, Kirkstone Pass, and Brothers Water, returning *via* the Vale of Troutbeck and Lowwood.

No. 12. Derwentwater (Keswick) Tour, *via* Ambleside, Grasmere, and Thirlmere.

No. 13. The Five Lakes Circular Tour, viz.:—Windermere, Rydal, Grasmere, Thirlmere, and Derwentwater.

No. 14. Wastwater Tour, *via* Seascale and Gosforth.

No. 15. The Six Lakes Circular Tour, viz.:—Windermere, Rydal, Grasmere, Thirlmere, Derwentwater, and Ullswater.

No. 16. The Duddon Valley Tour, *via* Broughton-in-Furness, Ulpha & Seathwaite.

No. 17. Levens and Heversham Tour, *via* Grange, Milnthorpe, and Arnside.

No. 18. Ennerdale Lake and Calder Abbey Tour, *via* Seascale, Gosforth, and Cold Fell.

No. 19. Across the Ferry Tour, *via* Esthwaite Water, Hawkshead, Ferry and Storrs Hall.

No. 20. Cartmel Priory and Newby Bridge Tour, *via* Windermere (Lake Side), Holker Park, and Grange.

Pamphlets giving full particulars of Fares, Trains, etc., can be obtained free of charge at all Furness Booking Offices.

The New Palette Album, illustrating the above Tours, can now be obtained at the principal Railway Bookstalls, price 6d.

Colourful posters were displayed at stations on the Furness Railway and were paraded through the streets of Blackpool on a hand-cart. The one illustrated here drew attention to the delights of Furness Abbey and some of the Lakeland beauty spots. There were also many concessionary fares including special tickets for golfers, anglers and tennis players. *7970*

Between the years 1902 and 1914 the Company produced for sale sets of picture postcards, as indeed did many other railway companies at that time, and surviving examples of these, together with all Furness Railway publicity items, are eagerly sought by today's collectors of railwayana.

TOURIST TICKETS

(Available for Two Calendar Months)

ARE ISSUED FROM

1st MAY to 31st OCTOBER,

From all the Principal Railway Stations to

Grange, Silverdale, Arnside, Kents Bank, Cark, Ulverston, Windermere (Lake Side), Bowness, Ambleside, Furness Abbey, Coniston Lake, Silecroft, Bootle, Ravenglass, Seascale, and St. Bees,

And holders of these Tickets are allowed to break their journey at any intermediate Station on the Furness Railway between Carnforth and their destination.

CHEAP WEEK-END and 10-DAYS TICKETS

ARE ISSUED

EVERY FRIDAY & SATURDAY

From the principal Manufacturing Towns in Derbyshire, Lancashire, Yorkshire, and the Midland Counties, to the Lake District and Furness Coast Stations, including Ulverston.

EXCURSIONS FROM AND TO LONDON.

DURING THE SUMMER

CHEAP EXCURSION TICKETS

Available by ordinary Trains are issued

From and to London and the Principal Stations on the Furness Railway,

TWICE A WEEK,

AVAILABLE FOR A WEEK OR A FORTNIGHT.

Attracting the tourist from the North, the Midlands and London.

The Outer Circular Tour

Above One of the most popular tours, and one undertaken frequently by holidaymakers from the Fylde coast resorts, was the 'Outer Circular Tour', and it is possible for us to take this tour now through the photographs in the Sankey Collection.

The poster illustrated here, which was displayed in the Blackpool and Fleetwood areas, gave prospective tourists a panoramic view of the delights of the Lake District and also offered, as an alternative to the tour - a three-hour return sea trip across Morecambe Bay to Barrow for only one shilling. *3210*

BLACKPOOL and the Lakes.

The Popular Paddle Steamers
'Lady Evelyn' or 'Lady Moyra'
SAIL BETWEEN
FLEETWOOD and BARROW
DAILY (including SUNDAYS)
from Whitsuntide until the end of September
IN CONNECTION WITH
Circular Tours & Day Trips to Lakeland.
Steamer Fares—Barrow (Ramsden Dock) & Fleetwood
SALOON: Single 2/6, Day Return 3/6.
FORE CABIN: Single 1/6, Day Return 2/6.

THE OUTER CIRCULAR TOUR			THE INNER CIRCULAR TOUR		
Embracing FurnessAbbey, Windermere Lake and Coniston.			Embracing FurnessAbbey The Crake Valley and Coniston Lake.		
FROM	1st	3rd	FROM	1st	3rd
BLACKPOOL	12/-	8/-	BLACKPOOL	9/6	6/-
FLEETWOOD	10/6	7/3	FLEETWOOD	8/-	5/3

For further information respecting the sailings of the Steamers, apply to Mr. A. A. Haynes, Superintendent of the Line, Barrow, or at all Furness Railway Stations; also at Messrs. Thos. Cook & Son's Offices and Agencies at Barrow, Blackpool. Fleetwood, Preston, Blackburn Bolton Burnley, Oldham, Rochdale, and Manchester.

Above Starting point for the tour was Talbot Road Station in Blackpool, jointly owned by the London & North Western and Lancashire & Yorkshire railway companies, which was built in 1898 to replace an original station on the Preston & Wyre Railway

dating from 1846. The twin-arched roof covered seven platforms, and the entrance, protected from the weather by the massive canopy seen in this photograph, was in Dickson Road. Seven excursion platforms, one of which would be used by the tour train, timed according to the poster to depart at 10.05 am, had a separate entrance. An early motor taxi, with Blackpool registration number FR 492 and sporting solid tyres, oil-lamps and an AA badge, waits under the canopy, while further down Dickson Road a Blackpool & Fleetwood Tram Company tramcar provides an alternative route to Fleetwood. *4400*

Above Fleetwood station, also under the joint ownership of the LNWR and L&Y companies, was situated adjacent to the steamer landing stages at the north end of the promenade, and it was here that tourists arrived from Blackpool to join the Furness Railway Company's paddle-steamers for the second stage of their outing.

The railway first arrived in Fleetwood in 1840 when the Preston & Wyre Railway Company opened a single line on 15 July, joining the port and holiday resort, founded by Sir Peter Hesketh Fleetwood

in the early 19th century, to the main railway network at Preston. *2174*

Below In the booking hall of Fleetwood station the ornate brick and ironwork associated with railway architecture can clearly be seen as station staff pose for Edward Sankey to take this photograph. The side frames of the porter's trolley on the left carry a reminder of the station's pre-LNWR/L&YR origins, proclaiming it to have once belonged to the P&WR. *2173*

Above Some idea of the popularity of the excursions can be gained by the size of this crowd waiting at the entrance to the Fleetwood landing stage to board the paddle-steamer for Barrow. *1652*

Below *Lady Evelyn*, well loaded with tourists, is nearing the end of her 1½-hour passage across Morecambe Bay from Fleetwood to Barrow. Photographed passing between Roa Island and Piel Island, with the ruins of the 14th-century Piel Castle visible beyond her stern, she is entering Walney Channel on her way to the landing stage at Ramsden Dock. *1666*

Above Entertainment during the crossing may have been provided by the small ensemble posing here, wearing the same uniforms and caps as the steamer's officers. This is a different group from the one that played in the Lakeside refreshment pavilion (see page 69) and on the lake steamers. *3680*

Below Another diversion for passengers was the visit of photographer Edward Sankey who, after travelling to Fleetwood on the early morning sailing, took group photographs of passengers on the return trip. On arrival at Barrow, while the passengers continued their tour the photographer returned to his darkroom, processed his negatives and made postcards for sale to the returning tourists on the early evening passage.

This elegantly dressed group was photographed on board *Lady Evelyn*, crossing from Fleetwood to Barrow, on 12 July 1911, and they would no doubt be eager to buy copies when the postcards were offered for sale on the return journey. Dressed in a fine array of fashions of the day, they seem determined to enjoy the outing, but the top-hatted, frock-coated gentleman in the background does not seem suitably attired for a day out in the Lakes.

Many of these group photographs, all titled with the name of the steamer and the date of the crossing, have survived, to be eagerly sought by today's postcard collectors. Unfortunately none of the negatives remain and this illustration is a copy of an original postcard.

Above Lady Evelyn arrives at Ramsden Dock at 11.45 am, coming alongside to tie up in front of *Lady Margaret*. Clearly visible at the masthead is the burgee carrying her name. For some reason *Lady Margaret* has her fore sail set. *652*

Below Ramsden Dock station had two lines of railway, one a through road and the other a bay, with an island platform between them on which was a refreshment kiosk. Standing in one of the platforms is 4-4-0 passenger engine No 124, waiting with a train to take the tourists on the next stage of their journey. Timed to leave at 11.55 am, the route was via Ulverston, Plumpton Junction and the Lakeside branch, arriving at Lakeside station at 12.50 pm.

No 124 was one of two similar engines ordered from builders Sharp, Stewart in 1900, the other being No 125. Becoming LMS No 10141 in January 1923, this locomotive was withdrawn from service for scrapping in 1928. *3218*

Above The schedule allowed time for lunch to be taken by those who wished to do so at Lakeside in the overhead verandah refreshment pavilion, at a cost of 2 shillings. During lunch Bateson's Orchestral Band would entertain diners between 12.25 and 1.25 pm every weekday 'free of charge' (see also page 69).

The dining room is seen here in its extended form, which dates the photograph as post-1906. *5114*

Below The landing stage, refreshment pavilion and station building at Lakeside recede into the distance as the steamer - in this instance either *Teal* or *Cygnet*, leaves for Ambleside at 1.35 pm.

Tied up alongside each other at the landing stage are *Swift* and *Tern*, while the steamer on the right is the other one of the *Teal/Cygnet* sisters. *9021*

Above On arrival at Ambleside the traveller changed his mode of transport yet again, forsaking the lake steamer for what must have been a much less comfortable means of conveyance. The journey from Waterhead to Coniston Station, made by horse-drawn charabanc, was, however, probably the most scenic part of the tour, passing first along the course of the River Brathay to Skelwith Bridge, then climbing over High Arnside and descending to Yew Tree Tarn before running through picturesque Yewdale to Coniston. An article in a contemporary magazine sets the scene as follows:

'The coach ride from Ambleside to Coniston forms an important part of the programme and when it is stated that on occasions 300 people make this tour at the same time, it will be seen that this number, although not large for the train or steamer, is important when coaching accommodation has to be provided, as many as 15 four- and six-horse coaches being required to carry so large a party.'

In this photograph a loaded four-horse coach, driven by a top-hatted coachman, is about to leave. As early as 1906, however, the internal combustion engine was seen as an alternative to the horse, and the Wolseley Tool & Motor Company offered to run a 30 hp motor omnibus between Coniston and Ambleside, to demonstrate that motor transport could be safely worked in connection with the tour. Wolseley offered to bear all expenses except the cost of fuel and lubricating oil, which had to be met by the Railway Company. There is, however, no evidence that this offer was ever accepted. *5195*

Left This later, post-1923, picture, including the landing stage and buildings at Ambleside, demonstrates that the internal combustion engine did indeed eventually take over from the horse to transport tourists away from the steamers.

Only one horse-drawn charabanc can be seen, compared with ten motor vehicles, and these include, on the left, a Dennis bus with the Westmorland registration number EC 8659, while in the centre the magnificent Daimler has Blackpool registration FR 4732. On the right an ice-cream cart belonging to T. Louie's of Kendal has been built on to a Model T Ford chassis with the registration B 7496. *D938*

Above The coach journey took 1¹/₂ hours to reach Coniston, where time was allowed for tea to be taken in the station refreshment room. This photograph, looking across the village, was taken from the top of the church tower and shows the station perched on the hillside in the background. The presence of the Railway Company's railmotor in the station dates the picture as between 1905 and 1908.

From Coniston, by a train leaving at 6.00 pm, the tourists travelled back to Ramsden Dock station via the Coniston branch and Foxfield, arriving at 6.55 pm. *2777*

Below After the early evening trip by paddle-steamer from Barrow to Fleetwood, during which they could collect the photographs taken on the morning crossing, the weary travellers arrived back in Blackpool at 8.45 pm, having been away nearly 11 hours. The fare for this tour from Blackpool in 1913 was 12 shillings 1st Class and 8 shillings for 3rd Class passengers. *4876*

The activities of the Furness Railway paddle-steamers were not confined entirely to the transport of holidaymakers between the Fylde coast and Barrow, and when the paddle-steamer *Lady Margaret* entered service on the cross-bay route in 1903, it was possible to experiment with alternative services using *Lady Evelyn*.

During 1903 a tentative service between Barrow and Morecambe, using the Midland Railway's pier at the resort, was initiated although sailings were limited by the fact that use of Morecambe Pier was subject to suitable tides. The service was inordinately successful, carrying 4,554 passengers paying £256 during a three-month season. When, during July, the tides at Morecambe were not favourable, *Lady Evelyn* returned to the Fleetwood service and the faster *Lady Margaret* was used to provide a Barrow to Southport service. This experiment was not so successful, however, the steamer carry-

ing only 851 passengers with receipts of only £71 during July and August, and as a result the service was cancelled.

There were also excursions to North Wales and the illustration shows *Lady Moyra* tied up at Menai Bridge during one of these. Two such trips are recorded; one on 11 August 1911 called at Southport, Llandudno and Bangor, carrying 2,668 passengers, obviously not all on the steamer at the same time, with receipts of £198. The success of this venture prompted another sailing to the same destination on Friday 9 August 1912, when 1,794 excursionists travelled, again on *Lady Moyra*. It is not known which of these two ventures is recorded by the photograph, but whichever it was, Edward Sankey went along and hired the small boat in the foreground to obtain his picture. His camera case can be seen in the boat, and the waiting figure is almost certainly his brother James. 2657

8.
FURNESS RAILWAY MISCELLANY

Signal boxes

Below left   This substantial brick-built signal box at Salthouse Junction opened on 12 October 1898, replacing a smaller box dating from 1888 (which can be seen in the enlargement of negative 6000 alongside). In an important location (see the map on page 32), it controlled movements on the main line between Barrow and Roose stations, access to marshalling and goods yards, docksides and gas works, in addition to the Stank mines and Piel branches.

Built to a standard design and similar to the one at Barrow Central North (see overleaf), Salthouse Junction box closed on 6 September 1992 when it was replaced by a ground frame, the only branch from the main line now being a single track serving the south side of Ramsden Dock. The box was demolished soon after the closure.

In this photograph the Piel branch curves to the right behind the box and the Stank branch leads from it in the forward direction, while the main line is on the extreme left. It is believed that the signalman looking out of the window was named Woodall. *7524*

Below right   An enlargement from the left-hand side of the Salthouse Halt picture (see page 71) shows that there were two signal boxes controlling the various lines merging at Salthouse Junction. The smaller one just to the left of the crossing's pedestrian gate dates from 1888, while the newer, larger box partially visible on the left is that pictured alongside. *6000*

Above Another substantial brick-built signal box, this time Barrow Central North, situated just beyond the northern end of platforms 2 and 3 at Barrow Central. It controlled not only trains entering

and leaving this end of the station, but also the carriage storage sheds and sidings, which were located at the northern end of the station, together with sidings leading to a timber yard and the Griffin Iron Ore Processing Plant. The structure in the photograph, opened on 8 September 1907, replaced a smaller box, similar in size and appearance to Barrow Central South box.

Despite its important role at what was undoubtedly the Furness Railway's principal station, Central North did not carry the highest rate of pay, the signalman in this box earning, in 1923, 60 shillings (£3) a week, as compared with the box at Barrow Loco Junction, which was rated at 65 shillings per week.

Central North signal box still exists almost exactly as it appears in this photograph taken in the early 1920s, except that the finial on the far end of the roof is missing, a casualty of the blitz of May 1941. Now known as Barrow in Furness North, the original frame, by F. W. Atkinson of London, is still in use, although less than half of the original 67 levers are now in operation. It is the last survivor from this manufacturer and each segment and lever is stamped 'FR'.

The diamond-shaped attachment on the wall below the open window, known as a telegraph board, denoted that the telegraph equipment was in good order and did not need the services of a travelling lineman. *7525*

Left A much smaller box than Central North, Central South controlled trains to and from the south together with sidings for several small industrial sites to the south of the station, including Barrow Electricity Works, Barrow Corporation materials storage depot and Briggs Foundry, a small works in Marsh Street. Despite its smaller size and the fact that it did not have the carriage sheds and sidings to control, it carried the same classification and rate of pay as Central North.

The illustrated wooden structure was replaced by a larger brick-based box, opened on 1 July 1928, situated on the south side of the bridge carrying Abbey Road over the railway. This later box disappeared in the late 1960s. *3701*

Above Opened on 17 August 1890, Loco Junction signal box combined the duties of three smaller boxes and controlled all movements into the locomotive shed and the Railway workshops complex. Such was its importance that it commanded the highest rate paid by the Furness Railway to any of its signalmen, 5 shillings per week more than any other box on the system in 1922.

Note the duster draped over the handle of the lever on which the signalman is leaning - an essential piece of equipment always in the signalman's hand when pulling levers. The levers themselves were painted in different colours, red for Home signals, yellow for Distants and black for points; white levers were spare. On the desk at the far end is the clock, and the box shows the customary clean and tidy state in which the signalmen always kept their workplace.

The lever frame is the Railway Signalling Company standard pattern as specified by the Furness in all signalling contracts placed from around 1896 onwards. Prior to this time, whenever new signalling equipment was needed, the chosen manufacturer's own

pattern was purchased, creating maintenance difficulties as parts were not interchangeable between frames and usually needed to be specially made for a location; this problem still exists. After this time frames were still purchased from a wide variety of suppliers, but being to a standard specification, although there were detail differences between frames, most parts were interchangeable.

The inside of this box is typical of those brick-built structures erected between 1896 and 1914. The lockers, for three men, would no doubt be made at the joiners' shop in Barrow Works, and similar examples to the single piece by the kitchen range are known to exist with 'FRC' stamped into them.

The plate on the front of each lever gives its number and function, as well as telling the signalman which other levers he will need to pull before the lever required will be released by the interlocking mechanism. The handle at the top of each lever, when gripped, lifts a block at the base of the lever over a raised shoulder on the frame, holding it in the reversed position.

The block instrument shelf above the frame is typical of those seen throughout the Furness system in the years leading up to the 1923 Grouping. The bell or gong would ring as the means of communication between the adjacent boxes, and the large wooden box beside the bell was the block instrument itself, which showed the state of the line to each adjacent location. Above this was the diagram showing the layout of all tracks under the signalman's control. The block instruments are of the Tyers one-wire three-position type, a system progressively introduced on the Furness from 1906 onwards, being rented from J. B. Saunders & Co, a firm of signalling contractors that was also responsible for their maintenance.

Loco Junction was unusual in that it had a secondary lever frame opposite the main frame. Much shorter than the frame on the left, some of the levers from this frame can be seen on the right of the picture.

Both frames were replaced by a modern British Railways standard frame during the 1950s, and Loco Junction box closed at the end of August 1970 after 80 years of operation. After a few years use as a shunters' cabin, it was demolished in the early 1980s. *3917*

Left The original signal box at Silecroft station, which opened on 14 August 1882, was, as can be seen in this photograph, of wholly wooden construction and not typical of boxes at Furness Railway country stations. The Up Starter signal on its lattice post is, however, of Furness origin, being the same as that at Furness Abbey station (see page 22). This wooden structure was replaced in 1923 by a new Furness Railway-designed box erected on the down side just south of the level crossing, which is still operational in its as-built condition. As a country station signal box, Silecroft was given classification 5 and wage rated at 50 shillings per week in 1922. *5568*

Wagons

Below left An enlargement from a negative recording the departure from Barrow of the battleship HMS *Vanguard*. Leaving through Ramsden Dock in October 1909 on her way to contractor's sea trials, she is passing an interesting line-up of Furness Railway ore wagons on the dockside.

The large, or 'jumbo', ore wagon is one of two built in America by the Pressed Steel Car Company and ordered in 1899, as an experiment, for transporting ore from the docks to Barrow Steel Works. Numbered 7534 and 7544 (the pictured wagon is 7534), they were some 22 feet in length and had a capacity of 45 tons of ore, which was discharged through drop doors in the bottom of the hopper-shaped body. There is no evidence that the company ever owned more than two of this type of ore wagon.

The smaller side-tippers, of which the Furness Railway owned a total of 314 with capacities of 7 and 10 tons of ore, were supplied by several builders, including S. J. Claye from its wagon works in Barrow. It is interesting to note that their buffers are set much lower than those of the 'jumbo', being only 3 feet above rail level as compared with 3 ft 5 1/2 in, making it impossible to mix both types of wagons in one train. A ruling in an Appendix to the Working Time Table dated 1 January 1905 states: 'Furness Tip Wagons on main line trains are always to be marshalled by themselves against the brake and are in no case to be run between ordinary sized wagons'. *805*

Top right The Private Owner Wagon, beloved of the railway modeller of today, was a colourful part of the railway scene prior to 1939, but with the pressure of wartime operating and the advent of nationalisation in 1948, the need for these vehicles to be always returned to their home depots became too restrictive and costly, with the result that their use was discontinued in favour of standard wagons owned by the railway.

This particular wagon, belonging to Barrow coal merchant Robert Balfour, whose offices were at 34 Strand, was photographed in Barrow goods yard, the building behind being in Hindpool Road (it can be identified in the picture on page 38). In an advertisement in the *Barrow Yearbook* for 1917 Robert Balfour offered for sale 'House and Steam Coals, Foundry and Gas Cokes' and would supply 'The Celebrated Haig Moor and Wallsend best house coals and nuts in bulk or bags to any part of the town at reasonable prices'.

Wagons such as this, built to a Railway Clearing House specification of 1907, were available from most wagon builders who could always supply from stock on receipt of an order. The illustrated wagon cannot be positively identified by the builder's plate above the left-hand axlebox, but records are available to demonstrate that it originated in the Motherwell works of Hurst, Nelson and Co, while the Ellis pattern grease axleboxes were made by Harrison & Camm of Rotherham.

All private owner wagons had to be registered by the local railway company and the registration plate between the brake pivot brackets in the centre of the sole bar shows this wagon to have been registered with the Furness Railway Company, number 452, to carry 10 tons. Fitted with side and bottom doors, the body would be in a red livery (which appears black on the ortho-chromatic photographic materials of the day) with white lettering shaded black to the left and below. *7707*

Middle left A close-up of a preserved Private Owner Wagon registration plate for vehicles with grease-lubricated axleboxes. *Geoff Holme collection*

Middle right A Private Owner Wagon registration plate for vehicles with oil-lubricated axleboxes. *Geoff Holme collection*

Bottom right A competitor taking part in a wagon-coupling competition in Barrow yard, with the side of the three-bay goods shed (seen in the picture on page 39) behind the wagons, which are of standard two-plank design, the one on the right being to Diagram 4 of 1899 and the one behind to Diagram 6 of 1906. It is on record that in 1907 the committee representing the competitors asked that the Company's annual subscription to the coupling competition be raised to 4 guineas, in order that a good prize could be offered in a competition to be open to all comers. The Company, through its Traffic & Works Committee, agreed to this request.

In the background are the chimney and accumulator tower that provided the hydraulic power to operate the dock gates and swing bridge at the northern end of Devonshire Dock. *RS5*

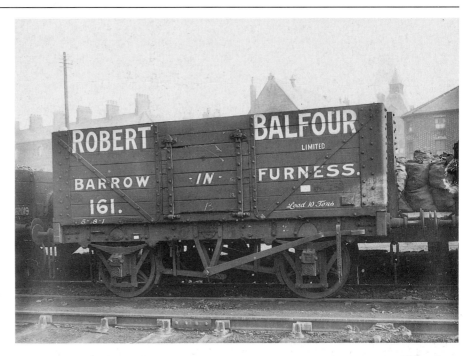

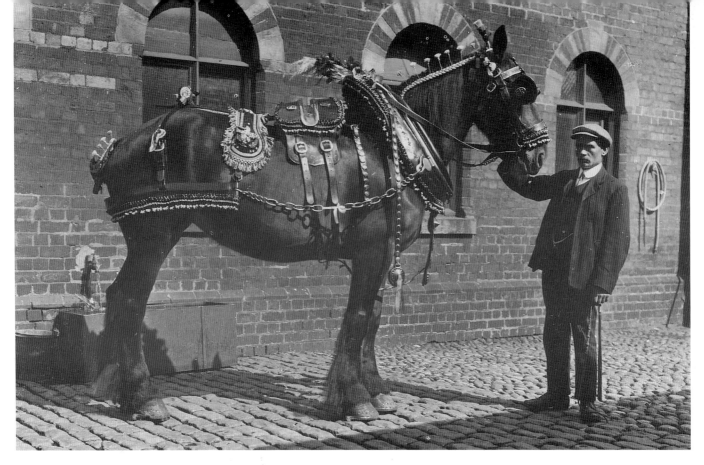

Road vehicles, etc

Above This picture is proof that the Furness Railway Company did not only operate 'iron horses'! It was reported that in 1912 the Furness Railway had 21 horses working on lorries, and here is one of them, immaculately groomed and decorated in full harness, posing with its proud handler in the Railway Company's stables. These were located in the Strand, close to the bridge carrying Michaelson Road across the High Level bridge on its way to Barrow Island; they still exist, although not now in railway ownership.

It is an interesting fact that the father of Edward Sankey, who took this photograph, was for some time in charge of the stables with responsibility for buying the draught horses needed to pull the Company's road vehicles. Also named Edward, he joined the Railway Company in 1863 as a parcels clerk at St George's Square at a wage of 20 shillings per week. *2284*

Below left The Furness Railway Company's exhibit in the Barrow Hospital Parade held on 11 September 1909 and possibly drawn by the decorated horse seen in the picture above it, was photographed, prior to the event, outside the Barrow Steam Laundry in Hindpool Road.

Consisting of a panoramic view showing industrial Barrow and the Lake District mountains, it incorporated an electrically driven model railway train, visible just to the right of the gentleman in the straw hat, encircling the float which could be illuminated at dusk.

Barrow Steam Laundry, according to its entry in a Furness Railway publication of 1900, held laundering contracts from Vickers Sons & Maxim Ltd, and the Railway Company. *2257A*

Above The possibility of replacing horse-drawn vans by motor vehicles for local parcel deliveries was first discussed in June 1902, when an estimate of £500 from the Wolseley Tool & Motor Co for a motor van, to be delivered in two years, was considered. However, after consultations with the General Manager of the Caledonian Railway, which was successfully operating motor vehicles, the matter was deferred, and the introduction of motor transport for the delivery of parcels seems to date from May 1904 when a 9 hp Milnes-Daimler van, registration number EO 40, was delivered.

At its meeting on 28 October 1912 the Traffic & Works Committee asked for tenders for the provision of a second motor vehicle, and that of the Albion Motor Company of Glasgow for a chassis costing £359 was accepted by the Board of Directors on 12 November of that year. The body of the vehicle was built in the Railway Company's own workshops at a cost of £25, and the blue and white vehicle, registration number EO 435, began service on 22 February 1913.

The purchase of the illustrated motor parcels van, registration number EO 1352, a 15 cwt Studebaker, at a cost of £270, was approved by the same committee at its meeting on Wednesday 31 May 1915. Replacing horse-drawn FR Parcels Van No 1, the new 20 hp vehicle was first registered on 16 June 1916, was painted dark blue and was photographed in front of the General Offices. It was scrapped in October 1928.

The Milnes-Daimler of 1904 was replaced on 17 January 1918 by a 30 cwt Whiting-Denby van, registration number EO 1591. In addition to these motor vans the Company also operated two motor goods lorries, a 30 hp Whiting-Denby, registration number EO 1158 dating from October 1915, and a 20 hp Ford, registration number EO 1698, bought in February 1919. *3999*

Below Another effect of the coming of the motor vehicle. *Geoff Holme collection*

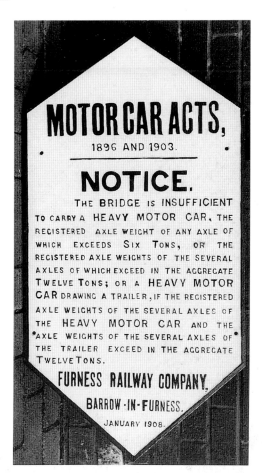

A Royal Visit

Above left On Thursday 17 May 1917, King George V and Queen Mary travelled to the North West to pay morale-boosting visits to Barrow and Workington, the major industrial towns of the region.

In this photograph the London & North Western Railway's Royal Train is seen at Furness Abbey station in the charge of two immaculately groomed Furness Railway 4-4-0 passenger engines, Nos 132 and 133, which had hauled the train from Lancaster.

Leaving Carnforth shed at 7.30, the two train engines and a pilot engine, coupled together, travelled tender-first to Lancaster, to take over the Royal Train at 9.00 am, Their Majesties having visited Manchester and Lancaster on the previous day.

Preceded by the pilot engine, running 15 minutes in advance, the special departed from Lancaster at 9.08 am, carrying an LNWR guard who had charge of the train as far as Carnforth. Timed to arrive at 10.00 am, the special drew into Furness Abbey a minute early, and here the Royal party alighted to begin their visit to Barrow. *7214*

Left King George, closely followed by Queen Mary, is seen on the platform after leaving the train, with a glimpse of the Furness Abbey hotel visible above the roof of the coach.

Waiting on the platform to be presented were a number of local dignitaries, amongst whom were a group of Furness Railway officials: Mr F. J. Ramsden, Chairman; Mr A. Aslett, General Manager; Mr W. F. Pettigrew, Locomotive, Carriage & Wagon Superintendent; and Mr A. A. Haynes, Superintendent of the Line.

After being driven along Abbey Road by motor car, pausing at the Town Hall for the playing of the National Anthem, the Royal visitors reached the works of Vickers Sons & Maxim at 10.25 am.

During the morning the King toured the engineering workshops, including the howitzer shop, while Queen Mary paid a visit to the Airship Shed at Cavendish Dock. After a light lunch in the General Offices, followed by a tour of the shipbuilding side of the works and

the new Shell Shop, Their Majesties were taken to see the airship building sheds on Walney Island, where local artist William McDowell was complimented by the King on his picture of Airship Number 9, which was on display.

At 1.00 pm the journey back to Furness Abbey began and the special train departed, on time, to take the Royal Party to their next engagement at Workington. *7216*

Above Shortly after the Royal visitors had left Furness Abbey station, the empty Royal Train ran on to Barrow Central, where it was stored until required to take the King and Queen on the next stage of their journey. Presumably during this period of inactivity the two train engines and the pilot would be serviced at Barrow shed.

It is interesting to note that the detailed special instructions regarding the working of the Royal Train, issued by Mr Haynes, ordered the special to run into platform 3 for storage, although this picture shows it in platform 4.

At 12.35 pm the train was reversed back to Furness Abbey, drawn by the pilot engine, tender-first, assisted by the two train engines, also tender-first, at the rear.

At 1.30 pm, with Their Majesties back on board, and preceded once again by the pilot engine, the special departed for Workington, where a visit to the Moss Bay Iron Works was planned.

With an LNWR guard on board, who took charge of the train from Whitehaven, Workington was reached at 3.15 pm. Here the Royal visitors disembarked and the empty train worked on to Brayton Junction, on the Solway Junction line, for storage. The Maryport & Carlisle Railway provided pilot drivers and guard for this part of the trip. The King and Queen spent the night on the Royal Train at Brayton before moving to Carlisle on Friday 18th for the final part of their visit to the North West.

Arrival at the storage point marked the end of the Furness Railway's involvement, and the two train engines left Brayton at 4.45 pm for Barrow shed, the pilot engine already having run on to Siddick for disposal.

Nos 132 and 133 were also used on the Royal Train when the King visited Barrow on 21 May 1915. *7218*

A couple of mishaps

Above At 7.45 on the evening of 20 February 1913 a collision occurred just north of Millom station in thick fog, when the 6.25 passenger train from Barrow was being shunted from the main line into the 1906-built carriage shed for overnight stabling. The 4.40 pm up fast goods from Whitehaven, headed by 0-6-0 goods engine No 8, passed a Home signal set at danger to protect the shunting operation, and crashed into the rear of the empty passenger train, derailing two coaches. The rear coach was flung on to its side, demolishing a signal box and damaging an adjacent wheel examiner's cabin, and the engine of the goods train was derailed. Mr J. Holmes, the signalman, escaped with cuts to his head, and but for the fact that he was pinned against the chimney by a piece of wood, might easily have been killed. Mr Jones, the wheel examiner, who was in his cabin at the time, escaped without injury, as did the driver and fireman of the goods train.

This photograph, taken on the morning after the mishap, shows the wrecked signal box and wheel examiner's cabin, with Millom station just visible through the overbridge on the right. The goods engine, which by this time has been re-railed, still blocks the up main line and trains from the north suffered delays, having to be worked with a pilotman on the down line into the station. *4023*

Below left A closer viewpoint shows clearly the wrecked signal box, its ivy-covered chimney still standing, the damaged wheel examiner's cabin and the offending locomotive which, uncoupled from its tender and without its connecting rods, has been re-railed. Note the basketwork 'swill' carried by one of the breakdown gang on the left, an indispensable piece of equipment for carrying practically anything by hand in pre-war days.

The official enquiry into the incident found that the driver of the goods train, which was travelling at only 10 mph when the collision occurred, was responsible in not having his train under proper control with regard to the unfavourable weather conditions, and despite hitherto having a good record, he was downgraded to shunting driver in Barrow Yard. The enquiry also referred to the position of the Home signal, which the Locomotive Superintendent considered was too close to the station siding where the accident happened, and suggested that it was moved some 60 yards further north. The Superintendent of the Line and the Engineer did not agree and the matter was referred to Mr Aslett. The wrecked box, dating from 15 June 1891, was rebuilt in timber, incorporating the original chimney and back wall, and reopened on 25 May 1913. *4025*

Above right Railwaymen engaged in the cleaning-up operation pose in front of the goods engine together with a police officer, who was probably there to keep spectators at a safe distance. The wrecked coach, which can clearly be seen in this photograph, was a five-compartment 3rd Class carriage with the running number 49, built in 1893 to Diagram 4 and seating 50 passengers. Valued at £450, it was so seriously damaged in the collision that it was decided to scrap it and replace it with an eight-compartment 3rd Class bogie carriage at an estimated cost of £1,000, the difference between the book value of the old coach and the price of the replacement being charged to capital. *4022*

Above This derailment occurred at the northern approach to Vickers Works, close to Walney Ferry signal box, which is just off the picture on the right-hand side, in North Road, Barrow. The line crossing the road in the foreground led to the dock gates of Devonshire Dock basin, which, until the opening of Ramsden Dock in 1879, was the entrance to the Barrow Docks system. The private owner wagons involved in the collision belong to the Featherstone Main Collieries of Yorkshire, which supplied coal to the Vickers Works.

In the background on the left the round-topped sheds that belonged to timber importers Burt, Boulton & Heywood, have now gone, and the site has become part of the submarine building hall of Vickers Shipbuilding & Engineering Ltd. *7028*

Strangers on the line

Above A coke train, hauled by London & North Western Railway 0-6-0 goods engine No 2227, pauses as it passes Lindal Ore Sidings on its way to Barrow Steel Works with fuel for the blast furnaces. The train includes wagons privately owned by Ferens & Love of the Cornsay Colliery at Durham, Grange Colliery in Yorkshire, and the Barrow Haematite Company. These trains from Durham, via the South Durham & Lancashire Union Railway, were usually taken over by Furness engines at Tebay, but there were a few workings from Tebay, during and just after the war, by LNWR locomotives, and this is presumably one of them.

The locomotive illustrated belonged to a large class of 0-6-0 goods engines, 310 strong, which were first introduced in 1880 and

which were curiously known as the 'Cauliflowers'. No 2227 had a long working life, being built in 1901 at Crewe and still being in service when the railways were nationalised in 1948, to become British Railways number 58427.

The lamp top on the wooden pole is typical of those to be found on stations and other locations throughout the Furness Railway system. The ground signals on the extreme right controlled movements in the sidings, rotating through 90 degrees to show a clear aspect. The steps on the left can still be seen today; note how the worn treads have been turned over and re-used. 5846

Below left Prior to the outbreak of war in August 1914, Britain's naval bases were located in the South of England and were supplied with all their needs by sea. But when the conflict with Germany began, the provision of bases in the north of the British Isles became necessary, in order to deal with the enemy threat from across the North Sea. As a result, the British Grand Fleet was moved to an anchorage at Scapa Flow in the Orkney Islands, where, because of the possibility of attack by enemy submarines, supply of stores, etc, by sea was dangerous. Rail transport was the obvious alternative and a great number of trains, many carrying coal to fuel the boilers of the warships based in Scotland, used the London & North Western Railway's main line over Shap on their way to Carlisle. On occasions, to relieve congestion on the Shap route, some of these trains were routed from Carnforth along Furness metals to Carlisle, and the blacked-out lamps at Seascale station, together with the LNWR 'DX' Class 0-6-0 locomotive at the head of a coal train, suggest a wartime scene, with the possibility that this is one of the 'Jellicoe Specials', as these trains were known. Clearly to be seen on the left-hand end of the platform building is the 1913-built refreshment room described on page 57. 5981

Right Maryport & Carlisle Railway 0-4-2 locomotive No 15, on its way to Barrow with a mail train, pauses briefly at St Bees station to collect from the frock-coated Station Master the token necessary to allow it to travel along the next single-track section to Nethertown. The first vehicle in the train is the Furness Company's 1902-built 35 ft 7 in Post Office Sorting Carriage, and the working timetable of 1 October 1918 shows this train, No 250, as a fast passenger leaving Whitehaven Bransty at 6.45 pm, calling at St Bees at 6.53 pm, and arriving in Barrow at 8.10 pm. There the Maryport & Carlisle locomotive left the train, which was taken on to Carnforth by a Furness engine. After a brief visit to Barrow shed for servicing, the M&C engine returned north hauling a fast through goods for Carlisle, leaving Barrow Yard at 9.50 pm and arriving in Carlisle at 2.55 am; this was train number 265.

Known to Furness Railway men as the 'Greenies' because of the colour of their livery, this particular engine was built at Maryport in 1892 and rebuilt in the form seen here in 1916. No 15 became LMS No 10012 in 1923, but was withdrawn, along with three similar engines, in 1928. Notice how low the station platform is in relation to the running plate of the locomotive - this was raised in 1920 at a cost of £500, and in the same year a footbridge was provided. 5933

Below A Furness Railway 0-6-0 engine in charge of a four-coach passenger train is seen here leaving High Harrington station on its way to Workington Central. High Harrington was not a station on the Furness Railway system, but was located on the Cleator & Workington Junction Railway, opened on 18 October 1879. This line ran from Cleator Moor Junction, on the jointly owned Whitehaven, Cleator & Egremont Railway, to Workington, with branches to Siddick, Linefoot, Distington, Rowrah and various iron and steel works in the Workington area. It was built primarily for the iron and steel trade, with only a limited number of passenger

services, and because of this the line was sometimes known as 'The Track of the Ironmasters'. The Distington to Rowrah section connected with the Rowrah & Kelton Fell Railway, a mineral line serving mines and a quarry producing iron ore and limestone for the large Glasgow firm of ironfounders, William Baird & Company, with the result that the branch was always locally called 'Baird's Line'.

Compared to other lines in the region, operated by the LNWR and Furness Railway companies, the Cleator & Workington Junction line was a very modest concern, and while it owned a small fleet of 0-6-0 saddle tank engines, serviced from a shed close to Workington Central station, most of the traffic was operated by the Furness Railway. The majority of the locomotives came from the nearby Furness shed at Moor Row, but a few were supplied from the small Furness-designed shed at Siddick. A large proportion of the goods stock and all of the passenger carriages were also provided by the Furness Company, the latter, because of the small number of passenger services, being mostly elderly six-wheeled coaches of the type seen in the photograph.

Passing into LMS ownership in 1923, withdrawal of passenger services began in the early 1930s, although freight traffic continued until 1964 when the line was finally closed. 6823

INDEX